How to Keep From Getting Hurt in the Church

By Dale A. Robbins, D.Min.

Victorious Publications
Grass Valley, California – Nashville, Tennessee
www.victorious.org

How to Keep From Getting Hurt in the Church
Copyright © 1995, 2015, Dale A. Robbins
Published by Victorious Publications
Grass Valley, California – Nashville, Tennessee
www.victorious.org

ISBN: 0964802228
ISBN-13: 978-0964802223

Other than where noted, scripture references are quoted from The New King James Bible, Copyright © Thomas Nelson Inc., 1979, 1980, 1982.

TLB - The Living Bible, Copyright © Tyndale House Publishers, 1971
NLT - New Living Translation, Copyright © Tyndale House Foundation, 1996, 2004, 2007, 2013
CEV - Contemporary English Version, Copyright © American Bible Society, 1991, 1992, 1995;
NIV - New International Version, Copyright © Zondervan, 1973, 1978, 1984, 2011
KJV - King James Version, Public domain, 1611

CONTENTS

	INTRODUCTION	v
1.	I'm Not Going to Let You Go!	Page 1
2.	Why Even Bother with the Church?	Page 9
3.	By This All Will Know You Are My Disciples	Page 22
4.	Avoid Developing Unreasonable Expectations of the Church	Page 32
5.	Don't Place an Absolute Trust in People	Page 38
6.	Focus on Common Ground	Page 47
7.	Don't Expect Any Church to Be Perfect	Page 52
8.	Don't Seek to Promote Yourself or Your Own Agenda	Page 57
9.	Avoid Blaming the Church for Personal Problems	Page 60
10.	Treat Others the Way You Wish to Be Treated	Page 67
11.	Have a Teachable and Cooperative Attitude	Page 72
12.	Don't Oppose or Hinder the Church	Page 78
13.	Be Committed to Forthrightness and Truth	Page 86

14.	Be Devoted to Love and Forgiveness	Page 95
15.	Don't Get Caught up in the Offenses of Others	Page 100
16.	Don't Personalize Everything That's Preached	Page 105
17.	How to Recover from Hurts You've Experienced	Page 111

INTRODUCTION

The title of this book may seem rather strange... weird in fact. After all, shouldn't a church be a safe haven for everyone? However, for many it hasn't always turned out that way. In fact, for some it's been a place of hurts and disappointments instead of hope, healing and spiritual direction.

I first began to address Hurts in the Church, through a series of sermons that I delivered years ago to various congregations I ministered to. I knew there was a widespread need for this kind of teaching, but was surprised by the popular response this topic received.

Then I wrote a series of articles that appeared in various publications, and which I published on the web by the same title as this book. In just the first few weeks, it was found and read by thousands from Google searches related to church turmoil and strife. It quickly became one of the most-read Christian articles on the web.

What is clear, hurts are common in the body of Christ everywhere, and are routinely exploited by Satan as diversions against the church. His ambition is to splinter and scatter the sheep if possible, to wound sincere believers and leaders, and to cause great harm to the work and mission of our Lord Jesus.

So what do we do? Despite our best efforts to avoid

contributing to hurts, we cannot prevent them from occurring entirely. We can only "preempt" Satan's mischief by becoming prepared and "immunized" in advance of what we know is inevitable.

Thus, the purpose of this book is to acknowledge that hurts and offenses will come to afflict all of us at some time or another *(Luke 17:1)*. But if we equip ourselves and each other with the wise instruction and counsel of the Word of God, such as what I've tried to present in this writing, we can resist their harmful effects and remain steadfast to our faith in God, and with our relationships in the body of Christ.

As most of us realize, America is at a crucial juncture in its history, and desperately needs a healthy, vibrant church to help light the pathway back to God. I pray that the things I've shared will help in that process... to help bring strength and wholeness to Christ's body, to best represent Him and serve His purposes in these last days.

May God use these principles to that end, and for His Glory!

Dale A. Robbins
Nashville, Tennessee

— 1 —
I'm Not Going to Let You Go!

"I will seek what was lost and bring back what was driven away..." (Ezekiel 34:16).

"Good morning, pastor," said the visiting couple as they entered our church sanctuary. I was delighted at their friendliness and replied eagerly. *"Good morning to you too... I welcome you to our fellowship... if you don't have a church home already, I hope we can become your new church family!"*

This young family was typical of many others who would visit our services each week but over the next few months, Tony and Lori along with their two children became regulars. I was ecstatic when they committed their lives to Jesus, especially since they were among our first new converts since I became pastor of the church. My wife and I were especially moved by Tony and Lori's sincerity, the genuineness of their faith, and enjoyed every opportunity to encourage and minister to them in their new relationship with Christ.

While pleased at their spiritual growth, I also became concerned with a variety of "thin-skinned" sensitivities that I began to detect with Tony, issues that I knew could possibly become potential offenses or setbacks in his future interaction with others in the church. There are not very many perfect people in any congregation (none in fact), and I knew it would only be a matter of time that someone could possibly say or do something that could wound or upset him.

This wasn't anything new, as I was accustomed to working with the many contrasting personalities of a congregation. Although one of our greatest goals for the church is to help followers of Christ develop a passionate love for Christ "and" for their fellow believers *(John 13:34-35)*, we pastors often have our hands full, keeping the peace and maintaining our focus while pursuing that goal. We teach people how to become loving and kind, so not to bring unnecessary wounds to others... while at the same time, teaching others how to become forgiving and "resistant" to the possible offenses that some might cause.

In Tony's case, he was a Christian "under construction," making great progress in his growth, but still young in the Lord. He was still touchy to a great many things, and with a history of blowing up and walking out of other relationships. My only prayer was that the roots of his maturity would deepen before having to encounter another believer as inversely "insensitive," or perhaps better described as "offensive," to the feelings of others such as himself. However, ready or not, the test came quickly... and the fireworks followed.

Tony had started performing as one of several musicians

in the worship band, and after their participation in an evening service, he got caught up in a heated argument with one of his fellow musicians, another fairly new believer. The next thing I knew, an usher came rushing to tell me that Tony had lost his temper with someone and was yelling that he was quitting the church. About that time, I spotted Tony, who had gathered his wife and children, and was stomping down the hallway toward the exit door. I called out to him, but he didn't respond... his face was red and frozen with anger.

My heart sank. He had been making such great progress. He and his wife, and each of his kids had all received Christ, had been baptized... and were growing in Jesus... and it appeared Satan was going to use this conflict to bring it all crashing down. My wife and I adored this brother and had invested our hearts in him and his family. But I knew from his past history, if we let him get out the door without resolving this ugly scene, he wouldn't be back... and I simply could not let this happen.

I followed him to the door, and called out again, *"Tony... please come back in, let's talk. Don't allow the Devil to get the victory in this situation!"* But he continued his march to the parking lot and to his car. A rain was just beginning to fall, and without thinking I rushed out and stood in the driveway as his car approached slowly. I kept calling to him, *"Tony, Tony... I love you... Jesus loves you,"* but his window was rolled up, and he wouldn't look at me.

Finally, although attired in my now soggy suite and tie, the Holy Spirit's presence came over me and I actually leaped up on the hood of his car, looked directly in his face through the windshield… and shouted, ***"Tony, I love you… Jesus loves you, and I'm NOT going to let you go!"***

At this, Tony applied his brakes, bowed his head to the steering wheel and began to weep and sob. I opened his car door, put my arm around him and we both wept and prayed… until he finally repented for his temper. I then asked him and the other brother together, both whom apologized mutually for their quarrel and divisive behavior. Praise the Lord!

This began a new phase of spiritual growth in Tony's life, and I'm glad to say that he and his family stayed with the church, and Tony grew spiritually and overcame most of these kind of issues. He and his family (including even the other gentleman) continued on with Christ for many years, until I departed that congregation and eventually lost touch.

In retrospect, at the time I gave no thought to whether jumping on his car's hood was the appropriate thing to do. It occurred to me later that this must have been a hilarious scene… certainly "not" the typical way a pastor should reach out toward those who have decided to leave the church!

However, in this instance, I believe the Holy Spirit knew this friend's soul was in danger. Tony wasn't just leaving to finding another church... he was parting ways with Jesus, and the Lord nudged me to take this drastic action. All I could think of was God's love… how God chased after me when I tried to run from Him so many years ago, and that His love would not let me go.

In the subsequent years thereafter, I thought about Tony often… and many other believers from the past whom I knew had been hurt, some who departed the church, or even ceased walking with the Lord for one reason or another.

And while I knew it was impossible to prevent all offenses from occurring in any church *(Luke 17:1-4)*, I also realized that pastors and ministers really must do a better job of anticipating such scenarios. I felt we needed to teach and equip believers to anticipate these issues... and to protect themselves, from allowing hurts, wounds or offenses to get the best of them.

As a result, I began a "proactive" approach of incorporating such teachings into our training for new converts and newcomers at their earliest entry level into our fellowship... and began to teach and write extensively on these issues at large.

Every believer, of course, should learn and understand the

biblical method of conflict resolution found in Matthew 18, in which Jesus taught how to resolve such matters "after" they occur (which we will discuss later). However, instead of waiting for an offense to come our way, why not prepare ourselves spiritually and load up on the stacks of scripture that teach how to prevent these issues "before" they occur?

"Conflict Preemption," as I call it, acknowledges that such encounters are not only possible, but are inevitable, and every Christian should study their Bible and prepare their hearts in advance of the hurts and wounds that are sure to come. As Benjamin Franklin once said, *"An ounce of prevention is worth a pound of cure."*

Pitfalls, Trials and Your Real Enemy

Living for Christ will never be without pitfalls, persecutions, trials and temptations *(1 Corinthians 10:13, James 1:2, 1:12, 2 Timothy 3:12)*... and our adversary, Satan, circles the flock 24/7 like a predator, looking for the weakest or most injured among us whom he can exploit and devour. *"Be sober, be vigilant; because your adversary the devil walks about like a roaring lion, seeking whom he may devour" (1 Peter 5:8).*

His method of operation is almost always "undercover," disguising his activities behind a shroud of people or things... invariably seeking to divert blame for his actions upon others. However, never forget who your "real" enemy is. It's not the church, not your brother or sister in Christ, nor is it the pastor. *"For we do not wrestle against flesh and blood, but against principalities, against powers, against the rulers of the darkness of this age, against spiritual hosts of wickedness in the heavenly places" (Ephesians 6:12).*

Satan and his wicked forces may not be directly responsible for every hurt or offense that pops up, but he certainly takes advantage of them all, and tries to find ways to magnify, exaggerate and make things seem worse than they really are.

Always remaining hidden in the shadows, the Devil constantly attempts to provoke mischief or stir up trouble where he can. He continually seeks careless words and stupid mistakes he can prey upon, always trying to deceive us into believing things that are not true. Don't buy into his lies and deceptions... neither allow yourself to blame fellow believers for the evil things he inspires or exploits.

Fortunately for us, Christ overcame the works of the Devil *(1 John 3:8)*, and passed on to us the same capacity to overcome him as well *(Luke 10:19-20)*. Since he is a "spiritual" adversary, we cannot combat him with earthly means, but only through spiritual weapons, as the Apostle Paul wrote, *"For the weapons of our warfare are not carnal but mighty in God for pulling down strongholds" (2 Corinthians 10:4).*

Paul encouraged believers to strengthen themselves in the Lord's power, to take on the spiritual "armor" he provides, to rise above the ploys and deceptions of the enemy. He said, *"...be strong in the Lord and in the power of His might. Put on the whole armor of God, that you may be able to stand against the wiles of the devil" (Ephesians 6:10-11 – Also study verses 12-18).*

Strengthen yourself in the Lord. Be quick to forgive, devote yourself to worship and prayer, don't abandon fellowship and keep your attention centered on the Word of God... that by His grace, He will keep you wrapped with His peace.

> ***"Great peace have they which love thy law: and nothing shall offend them." (Psalms 119:165 KJV)***

— 2 —
Why Even Bother with the Church?

"And let us not neglect our meeting together, as some people do, but encourage one another, especially now that the day of his return is drawing near." (Hebrews 10:25 NLT)

Before going any further, the question arises, why should anyone even consider gathering with a church where hurts or offenses might possibly occur? Why not just avoid such congregations, or stay home entirely and eliminate these kinds of risks completely?

Unfortunately, this is exactly what millions of Americans have already decided to do. However, abandoning the fellowship of the church can bring about detrimental effects to one's faith and relationship with God, and it's definitely not Christ's plan or desire for any believer to give up on His church.

While there are terrific churches to be found in most communities across America, unfortunately there are also exceptions… that have sometimes contributed to needless hurts and offenses, perhaps by fighting or quarreling over nonessential matters, wrestling for power or control, allowing or enabling exploitation by corrupt members or leaders. (Sounds kinda like Washington Politics, doesn't it?)

It's regrettable that such dysfunctions ever occur... but this kind of instability is not typical of all congregations, and shouldn't be used as an excuse to abandon the church.

If you have a bad church experience like this, obviously, seeking a new church home may become an option, but never make church changes quickly, often or lightly. Certainly, don't act without first making it a serious matter of prayer. Remember, the church is not a building or a location, but rather, the body of Christ, the followers of Jesus. And even if the Lord directs you to fellowship elsewhere, it must be done with love, courtesy and respect.

However, if you continue to experience hurts, offenses or conflicts in a variety of other churches you attend, then maybe the problem isn't the church at all. Perhaps "you" have issues, sensitivities or preferences of your own that may need adjusted or "humbled" with regard to your expectations, or with how you interface with the church or the congregation. This is the greatest reason why there is so much discontent with churches... which we will address in this book.

The Presence of God in the Church

Although there is no specific verse that exactly says "Thou shalt attend church every Sunday morning," we know that continuing to come together with the body of Christ is the Lord's plan for many reasons.

Besides going to hear preaching and teaching of the Word that will help increase your faith and keep you on the right track with God *(Romans 10:17, Ephesians 4:11-13)*, it also provides you opportunities to honor, serve and worship the Lord together with other believers *(Acts 2:46-47, Hebrews 10:24-26, Matthew 18:19-20),* and to combine your talents and resources to accomplish tasks and missions for the Lord's kingdom *(Leviticus 26:8).*

But perhaps the most extraordinary reason why we need to get together with the church, is the promise that the Lord makes to those who gather. He pledges a special visitation of His presence "in the midst" of them... and assures that He will honor their prayers of agreement. The scope of this guarantee is really phenomenal, and if anyone believes in and values the presence of God, they cannot afford to ignore what Jesus said:

> ***"I say to you that if two of you agree on earth concerning anything that they ask, it will be done for them by My Father in heaven. For where two or three are gathered together in My name, I am there in the midst of them." (Matthew 18:19-20)***

As amazing as this promise is, however, there is a deeper truth about this "gathering" that is often missed... which deals with the word "together." To explain, this is not merely a gathering, but a "gathering together," a reference pointing toward a unity and "togetherness" of those assembled in the name of our Lord Jesus.

What this reveals is that the Lord not only wants to be worshiped by persons who have a devotion and passion for Him... but also for <u>each</u> <u>other</u>. We can see an example of this by the union He portrayed between Himself and His disciples at the Last Supper. There He taught that all believers are merged together as members of His body, the church... something that brings importance to the idea of fellowship and harmony, in order to bring wholeness and completion to the body of Christ.

When this "vertical" and "horizontal" fellowship occurs between the Lord Jesus and His followers, it especially pleases and honors Him. He not only promises to answer the agreed-upon prayers of such a group, but assures that He will manifest His presence in an extraordinary fashion, "in the midst of them." Perhaps this meaning is similar to the day of Pentecost, when the Holy Spirit's presence came mightily upon those who were gathered *"with one accord in one place" (Acts 2:1)*.

This is certainly a worthy sacrifice of your time and energies, to gather with the church so to invoke the Lord's presence... not only for your own blessing, but also for the benefit others will receive from your contribution to the gathering. In other words, even if you can pretend that you have nothing to gain by going to church... it's still worthwhile to go, to lend your support to the gathering, out of your love, care and respect... both for the Lord Jesus, and for fellow brothers and sisters in Christ.

Your Need for Fellowship

"But if we walk in the light as He is in the light, we have fellowship with one another, and the blood of Jesus Christ His Son cleanses us from all sin." (1 John 1:7)

Gathering together unto the Lord Jesus is essentially what the idea of "fellowship" is all about. The scripture says that "fellowship with one another" is the normal expectation of "walking in the light," a frequently used metaphor by John, referring to living in a right relationship with Christ. *"I am the light of the world. He who follows Me shall not walk in darkness, but have the light of life" (John 8:12).*

In modern church vernacular, fellowship generally refers to the concept of "socializing," such as activities, dinners or social events, insomuch that many churches even have rooms, buildings or gymnasiums dedicated to fellowship activities.

However, "fellowship" *(κοινωνία or koinonia)* has a more substantial spiritual meaning... relating to the spiritual relationship that connects all believers to Christ and to each other. This common bond exists by the mere status of our faith in Christ... but is "practiced" by engaging in intimate gatherings with fellow believers, to share and express mutual love, support and encouragement in Christ.

The Last Supper and the Body of Christ

The basis for this fellowship was introduced by Jesus at His Last Supper with His twelve Apostles, the night before His trial and crucifixion. Jesus served bread and wine as symbols of his broken body and shed blood, to show that his sacrifices were necessary sustenance for spiritual life, which all believers must partake of by faith. It was also to illustrate that those who receive His redemptive sufferings by faith, would share a "spiritual union" or *koinonia* between Himself and all other believers.

As the Apostle Paul described, *"The cup of blessing which we bless, is it not the communion (koinonia) of the blood of Christ? The bread which we break, is it not the communion (koinonia) of the body of Christ? For we, though many, are one bread and one body; for we all partake of that one bread" (1 Corinthians 10:16-17).*

After the events of that supper, the term "body of Christ" would no longer belong solely to the physical anatomy of Jesus, but to the merged relationship between Himself and His believers, the church. A spiritual union between Jesus and His followers became a reality, allowing Him to go to the cross as our substitute, *"who Himself bore our sins in His own body on the tree" (1 Peter 2:24)...* while also enabling us to become His hands, feet and body... the body of Christ on the earth, as Paul later wrote, *"Now you are the body of Christ, and members individually" (1 Corinthians 12:27).*

Following the resurrection of Jesus on that first day of the week, the Lord's Supper became a regular observance in the weekly gatherings of the church, consisting of *"...the apostles' doctrine and fellowship (koinonia), in the breaking of bread, and in prayers" (Acts 2:42).* Not only did these gatherings maintain the idea of *"koinonia"* as Jesus had emphasized, but were so focused on loving one another, that they were actually called *"Agape" (ἀγάπη)* or *"Love Feasts" (Jude 1:12).*

The Value Jesus Places on Fellow Believers

Today, as sacred as most Christians view the symbols of Christ's bodily sufferings from the Lord's Supper... there are many others who remain oblivious to the fact that Jesus was depicting a spiritual integration of all of His followers into unified relationship with Himself. He explained and illustrated how that all who believe and spiritually ingest His redemptive sufferings in behalf of their sins, become a member of His sacred body, the church.

In other words, while most Christians appropriately recognize the sacredness of Christ's bodily sufferings in their behalf, there is often an insufficient recognition or "value" extended toward what "Jesus" considered to be sacred and precious... namely, our fellow brothers and sisters for whom He sacrificed Himself to redeem. (This issue may very-well contribute to what Paul described as an inadequate discernment of the Lord's body, 1 Corinthians 11:29.)

Imagine for a moment, if you could place some measurable value upon Jesus Christ... an appraised worth of the sufferings and sacrifice that He gave by His death on the cross. What would your value be? Someone estimated the total monetary value of the world to be somewhere over one quadrillion dollars, $1,000,000,000,000,000, which would be equal to a thousand trillion, or a million billion dollars. Would "that" be an equitable worth to the atonement of Jesus Christ? Hardly.

Obviously, as you and most Christians would probably

agree, the redemptive value of what Jesus did for us, as well as for every human being on earth, is priceless… worth far more than all the wealth of the universe. **Yet, this infinite value is what Jesus placed on <u>you,</u> and on <u>each</u> <u>believer</u>, by paying the price of His own death and sufferings on your behalf.**

> *"…I live by faith in the Son of God, who loved me and gave Himself for me." (Galatians 2:20)*

This appraisal of Jesus' sufferings helps us understand something about the idea of "Love." Love involves a "value" that we place on something or someone. When we express our love to someone dear, we often describe "how much" they mean to us… how much we "treasure" them… or perhaps make comparisons to other valuable things, such as "I love you more than all the stars in the sky."

Likewise, "acts" of love are based on values, such as giving an expensive gift to someone who means a lot to you… or forfeiting your time from doing something important, in order to spend those moments with your wife, your children or those you love.

And of course, the greatest treasure that any of us have, is our own life… which is why Jesus explained that there is no greater love, than for a person to spend his most valued possession in behalf of another. *"Greater love has no one than this, than to lay down one's life for his friends" (John 15:13).*

So, considering Christ's extraordinary love, insomuch that He willingly laid down His life for you and all those who have followed Him... what kind of value "do you" place upon those whom Christ died for? In other words, if Jesus has placed such a high value on your brothers and sisters in the Lord... what are they worth to you?

This is an important question, because the value you place on your fellow believers, reveals how much love you have for them.

> **"By this we know love, because He laid down His life for us. And we also ought to lay down our lives for the brethren" (1 John 3:16).**

Let Us Consider One Another

What we discover is that the issue of "one another" is very important as it pertains to the church, and upholds what is probably the strongest scriptural argument for why you shouldn't give up on church.

On that basis, let's look at the one scripture passage that says the most about the believer's duty to assemble together... and why it's so crucial:

> ***"And let us consider one another in order to stir up love and good works, not forsaking the assembling of ourselves together, as is the manner of some, but exhorting one another, and so much the more as you see the Day approaching. For if we sin willfully after we have received the knowledge of the truth, there no longer remains a sacrifice for sins" (Hebrews 10:24-26).***

As you can see, the writer plainly explains, *"Don't stop assembling together like some have done,"* which in light of the trends today, sounds like it could have been written last week. And note carefully the emphasis on "why" you should not abandon the church meetings.

The motivation in this instance doesn't focus on "you" or about "your" spiritual needs, but rather upon the needs of "others." He says to "consider one another." For what reason? Besides what we already mentioned, to invoke Christ's presence… and to **encourage them, and find ways to motivate and inspire their love and good works in Christ.**

Gathering together is essentially how a believer practices love toward other believers. Sure, you can love and worship the Lord from home… or express loving sentiments toward others in your thoughts, or by phone, letters or email… which are the next-best alternatives when it's not possible to be there with the people of God. But these virtual methods can never replace your personal presence with the church, to love and encourage one another through fellowship.

Love can be understood as a condition of one's attitude toward another, perhaps contained in sentiments of kindness, value, affection… but Agape love (God's kind of love) is not meant to remain only as a "noun," but to become active as a "verb." Brotherly Love is not just a matter of good sentiments toward Christians, but it's a matter of doing something, acting on those sentiments… by engaging each other, blessing and encouraging, giving and sharing, by putting their needs above your own… worshiping and honoring the Lord together.

How many people do you suppose actually think that going to church is about being a blessing or encouragement to others? Some yes, but I can attest from my many years as a pastor, the greatest bulk of Christians think it's only about themselves. "I should to go to church so 'I' can hear God's Word, so 'I' can Worship, so 'I' can be blessed and strengthened in 'my' faith."

Of course, there are plenty of other important reasons why you should gather with the church, but none more compelling than to love one another. The greatest impetus for assembling with the body of Christ, should be out of your love and consideration for God and your fellow believers… so you can bless, inspire, and encourage them in the Lord Jesus.

The bottom line is, besides your devotion for Christ, your love toward "one another" is the greatest reason for coming together with the Church. There are Christians who need your love… but perhaps more importantly, you need them to practice your love.

— 3 —
By This All Will Know You Are My Disciples

"A new commandment I give to you, that you love one another; as I have loved you, that you also love one another. By this all will know that you are My disciples, if you have love for one another" (John 13:34-35).

"Love" is known as the great Christian "commandment" of our Lord Jesus Christ. It is not a suggestion, but rather His "requirement" for believers to love each other, as He loved them… a trait so important that Jesus said that it would be convincing proof to the world that we are truly His followers.

I always found this passage from John interesting, to consider why Jesus saw the importance for the world to observe "Christians loving Christians." We naturally assume that the world will know that we are His followers if we show our love to "them." However, Jesus seemed to say that our "love for one another" is necessary for them to observe… perhaps suggesting that skeptics need to see how we treat each other first, before they buy into the idea that we love them too.

Not only is love commanded by Christ, serving as

universal proof that we're his disciples… it's also what John described as "our own" evidence of salvation, as seen in this passage below:

> ***"We know that we have passed from death to life, because we love the brethren. He who does not love his brother abides in death. Whoever hates his brother is a murderer, and you know that no murderer has eternal life abiding in him." (1 John 3:14-15)***

The first line of this verse is so substantial, we should memorize it, underline it in our Bible… and perhaps print it out and post somewhere so we can never forget it. Here's how the New Living Translation puts it. *"If we love our Christian brothers and sisters, it proves that we have passed from death to life. But a person who has no love is still dead" (1 John 3:14 NLT).*

Simply stated, there are no alternatives to the necessity of brotherly love. Believers must love other believers, Period. The absence of that love, indicates the presence of spiritual death. But also understand, this kind of love is not something you can produce of yourself… nor is it something you must do to earn approval from God. Love for other believers is simply the evidence of Christ's love dwelling inside you. *"Beloved, let us love one another, for love is of God; and everyone who loves is born of God and knows God. He who does not love does not know God, for God is love" (1 John 4:7-8).*

How Loving One Another Affects Us

Here below is another powerful passage that draws a comparison between our relationship with God and with our fellow believers... but with an added caveat:

"Since you have purified your souls in obeying the truth through the Spirit in sincere love of the brethren, love one another fervently with a pure heart." (1 Peter 1:22)

Again as with other verses, Peter associates our spiritual condition with our love for the brethren... however, in this case he also suggests that such love, resulting from obeying the Spirit of truth, has caused a "purifying effect" on our souls... to which, he encourages the further progress of this effect, by pouring on "fervent love" toward each another with a pure heart.

This isn't the first time we've seen this similar association. 1 John 1:7 appears to suggest a correlation between fellowshipping with one another and the continued cleansing of our sins. And remember the purpose of assembling together in Hebrews 10:24-26? He warns us to not stop meeting together... lest this leads to willful sin and apostasy.

And finally, we come to another profound verse that combines and builds on what we've already shared, by adding that loving our brethren is not only evidence of a right relationship with Christ (walking in the light)... but also helps build a "spiritual immunity" against the sins that can trip us up:

"He who says he is in the light, and hates his brother, is in darkness until now. He who loves his brother abides in the light, and there is no cause for stumbling in him." (1 John 2:9-10)

This of course, ties together closely with what John wrote just a chapter earlier, stating that fellowship with one another has a relationship to the continued cleansing of sin, the result of (walking in the light) a right relationship with Christ:

"But if we walk in the light, as he is in the light, we have fellowship with one another, and the blood of Jesus, his Son, purifies us from all sin." (1 John 1:7 NIV)

You Need Somebody to Love

While writing this, my thoughts reminisced back to the lyrics of an old Jefferson Airplane song, "Don't you need somebody to love." Although their intended message back then was something quite different, the words coincide and resonate with our message here. Not only is it the Lord's command... but "you need somebody to love" in Christ, because it does something for you spiritually that cannot be accomplished any other way.

Basically we need brothers and sisters in Christ to love, in order to maintain a right relationship with God. We can't love Jesus any more than we love the members of His body, or what He called the church.

> ***"...for he who does not love his brother whom he has seen, how can he love God whom he has not seen?" (1 John 4:20).***

Fellowship with our brethren is an exercise of love that God uses to help develop our spiritual maturity. Your relationship with the brethren is a thermometer that measures your spiritual temperature. Your degree of love toward the body of Christ is the gauge that shows your love for God. *"...If we love one another, God abides in us, and His love has been perfected in us" (1 John 4:12).*

Fellowship with the body of Christ is where love is tested and proven. It is the opportunity to learn how to love one another, and is God's great classroom of the development of Christian character. We are benefited by both, the strengths and weaknesses of the fellowship. The mature ones help to strengthen and encourage us, while the weaknesses in the less mature, give us the opportunity to "practice" or to "test" our spiritual growth... especially in such characteristics as patience, long-suffering, gentleness, meekness, etc. (All spiritual virtues must be challenged and tested to bring forth progress.)

And at some time or another, you'll probably meet a few

(or maybe many) rude, offensive or immature believers in the body. They need someone like you to show them love and patience (so they'll grow up), but you also need them in order to practice and develop your love for the brethren. When you can remain loving and steadfast, even though disappointed by brothers who say negative things about you, or let you down, or do offensive things… your love is being perfected… and you're growing up as a Christian and becoming more like Jesus Christ!

The truth is, you can't love the Lord any more than you love the body of Christ, His church. We have all become members of His flesh, partakers of His blood… as previously shown to us through the Lord's supper, as well as other instances. One of which is the story of Saul, who prior to his conversion (renamed as Paul), went about persecuting, arresting and even murdering Christians *(Acts 9:1-3).*

So when Jesus appeared to Saul in a blinding light on the road to Damascus, do you remember what Jesus asked him? He said, *"Saul, Saul, why are you persecuting Me?" (Acts 9:4-5)* Saul, however, was not persecuting Jesus personally, but only His "followers"… so what did Jesus mean by that? Well, as far as Jesus is concerned, what's done against one of His followers, is done against Himself… because they are members of His body.

This therefore explains why we cannot repudiate anyone

who is truly a member of Christ's body. As Paul later wrote to Christians, *"Now you are the body of Christ, and members individually" (1 Corinthians 12:27).* How can you reject any person whom Jesus has accepted… and made part of Himself?

Jesus takes personally, how you treat your brothers and sisters in Christ. This is what Jesus meant in his parable of separating the sheep from the goats:

> ***"Assuredly, I say to you, inasmuch as you did it to one of the least of these My brethren, you did it to Me." (Matthew 25:40)***

Who might be considered the "least" of your brothers and sisters in Christ? Could these be persons of a different race or color who sit on the other side of the church from you? Could these be the ones who appear disheveled, poorly dressed, or even smell of foul body odor? Or could it be those followers of Jesus who attend a different church, a different denomination, or who worship slightly different than yourself?

Christians don't have the privilege of choosing who they will, or will not love. While we do have a right to withhold "trust" toward anyone, until we can attest to their character, faith and relationship to Christ… we must love and accept those that Jesus loves and accepts… without partiality *(James 2:8-9).*

Picking and choosing whom we think is worthy of our love and fellowship in Christ's body, is a type of religious bigotry... or what is sometimes called being a "respecter of persons." For this reason, "cliques" formed within a church with the intent to exclude others, can cause many hurts and feelings of rejection.

Jesus doesn't only love the popular ones, who are fit, youthful, attractive, wealthy... but He loves us all, including the "least" among us, with no regard to our appearance, intelligence, affluence or importance.

So is Church Really Necessary?

As I've shared with you now at great length... as a follower of Jesus Christ, YES, it is necessary and important for you to participate with a local fellowship of believers... that is, if you're sincere about following Jesus, and serious about wanting to go to heaven. The body of Christ needs you, and you need them... to practice your love, to obey and honor the Lord, to manifest the presence of Christ... as well as to honor and worship the Lord together, to grow in your knowledge and faith, and to combine your strength to accomplish tasks and missions for God's glory.

Someone once asked me... *"What good can it do for me, to come to church and worship God with a bunch of idiots?"* Well, besides the fact that your loving such "idiots" may help provide proof of whether you're really saved or not, they may also allow you an opportunity to grow up in spiritual maturity, by developing such characteristics as mercy, kindness, forgiveness, humility, gentleness, patience, encouragement etc.

Jesus died for "idiots"…just like you and me, so the more you come to love His people, even with their flaws and shortcomings, the more you will come to know Him and become like Him:

> *"Dear friends, let us practice loving each other, for love comes from God and those who are loving and kind show that they are the children of God, and that they are getting to know Him better. But if a person isn't loving and kind, it shows that he doesn't know God – for God is love." (1 John 4:7-8 TLB)*

So if you've been hurt by the church, or by some of the "idiots" there, please don't run away, but equip yourself with the protection of God's Word that I'll share in the remaining chapters. Seize the opportunity to love, to forgive, and to grow in maturity… to help make the church a stronger and more mature fellowship for everyone.

> *"Therefore, as the elect of God, holy and beloved, put on tender mercies, kindness, humility, meekness, long-suffering; bearing with one another, and forgiving one another, if*

anyone has a complaint against another; even as Christ forgave you, so you also must do. But above all these things put on love, which is the bond of perfection. And let the peace of God rule in your hearts, to which also you were called in one body; and be thankful. Let the word of Christ dwell in you richly in all wisdom, teaching and admonishing one another in psalms and hymns and spiritual songs, singing with grace in your hearts to the Lord." (Colossians 3:12-16)

— 4 —
Avoid Developing Unreasonable Expectations of the Church

"My soul, wait silently for God alone, For my expectation is from Him." (Psalms 62:5)

Now that we've laid a stronger foundation of why you need the church, you also need God's Word to help "immunize" yourself against the potential hurts, offenses or pitfalls you may find there.

One of the first issues that I usually address toward this immunization process, is the matter of "false expectations." In other words, you must avoid expecting things from a church or its pastor that they can't deliver… or that the Bible doesn't teach them to do. Many disappointments with the church often begin with unfulfilled expectations based on a variety of anticipated customs or traditions, or perhaps from our past experiences in another congregation that we once attended or grew up in, etc.

What we may not understand is that traditions vary from church to church, or from pastor to pastor. So whenever starting to attend a particular church, it's a good idea to find out exactly what they believe and how they handle issues that might be important to you. Meet with the pastor or church leaders to clarify your understanding of how the church is operated and what can be expected from their ministry.

It's also advisable for every church to "preempt" such misunderstandings by having a clear "ministry statement" with an explanation of what attendees or members can expect. Otherwise, if left to the imagination, people can cook up almost any kind of demands or expectations from the church... things I never dreamed they might expect, prior to my years of service as a pastor.

For instance, occasionally there are those who think of the church as a type of government assistance program. While it is true that most ministers and churches attempt to help the needy, especially during crises and emergencies, it is not realistic to expect a church to supply all of a person's material needs, or to pay their bills like the early church did. Unfortunately, this isn't possible unless everyone will voluntarily sell all their property and possessions, and give them to the church to disperse to the poor, as did the initial believers *(Acts 4:34-35)*. Most churches would be blessed if everyone merely paid their tithes, however only a small percentage of churchgoers contribute a full tithe regularly in most churches.

Other typical disappointments might stem from the inability of the pastor to socialize or spend a lot of personal time with church members. This again is may depend on the tradition of the particular pastor or perhaps the size of the congregation. Obviously, in order to effectively "minister" to persons, any pastor is wise to make personal connections and fellowship with his congregants as often as possible. However, it's unreasonable to think the pastor can spend all his free time with you or attend every social function. Pastors have many demands on their time that congregants often do not realize.

Another frequent disappointment often deals with political issues and power struggles within a church. Contentions about how the church is run, or persons who strive against one another for influence or control. This often may also involve controversies over favoritism, cliques and nepotism, how the money is spent, etc. Foolish squabbles like this are among the top reasons many people give up going to church. The best thing is to steer clear of churches that are ruled by things like this to begin with. But to avoid hurts and disappointments in any church, you should bypass anything that smells like contention, strife or politics.

What can be typically expected from your church? First of all, understand that a local church is not merely an organization or a building, but a fellowship of believers who gather to worship God and to grow in their faith and relationship with the Lord Jesus Christ.

It's nice if the music is flawless, the seats are padded or

the minister dismisses promptly at noon. But more importantly, we need a church that cares about us and will help meet our spiritual needs – that will inspire us to grow toward the aspirations of God. We need a pastor whose preaching and teaching will not merely appease or entertain, but will boldly challenge us to advance beyond comfort zones to live toward God's high ideals. These characteristics are more important than his eloquence, education or charisma.

Ideally, We Should Expect Our Church to Be Striving Toward These Goals:

(1) To minister to our spiritual needs, by teaching and upholding the truth of God's Word, the Bible.

(2) To be "Christ-centered" and focused on the mission of drawing people closer toward a personal relationship with Jesus Christ.

(3) To exhibit and inspire love for the Lord and for one another.

(4) To embrace and uphold good Christian character, with pastors and leaders devoted to godliness, prayer and the Word.

(5) To be a peaceful, stable environment where you and your family can be loved and accepted...

as well as forgiven and restored should you fail or stumble.

(6) To be seeking to reach lost souls... attempting to bring lives to Christ, both in their community and on foreign mission fields.

(7) To provide opportunities for service where you can get involved... by serving, giving and reaching out to others in ministry.

If you're not part of a church that has these basic qualities, you should find one that does. And if your church "is" anything like what we've described, you then should be thankful to God for the opportunity to be a part of such a blessed fellowship. You should avoid becoming discontent or distracted over superficial issues that have nothing to do with the more substantive ideals of the church.

Ultimately, the objective of the church is not to draw your focus or expectations on itself, but to lift your attention up to the Lord Jesus Christ, where all your expectations can be safely and confidently directed. People can fail us... as well as the organization of the church, or its leaders, pastors or members. However, the Lord Jesus will never fail! He will always be faithful to honor your faith and the promises in His Word.

Consequently, placing your expectations in "the Lord,"

rather than the church, it's people or leaders, is an important key to avoiding wounds, offenses and disappointments in the church.

— 5 —
Don't Place an Absolute Trust in People

"Thus says the LORD: Cursed is the man who trusts in man and makes flesh his strength, whose heart departs from the LORD." (Jeremiah 17:5)

When Jeremiah uttered this prophecy regarding Judah's sins and impending judgment, he reminded them of what brought their downfall. They had turned away from their former trust and reliance upon God, and chose instead to look toward mortal and earthly alternatives for their values, beliefs and solutions. A classic portrayal of a backslidden society. (Such as we face today in the United States.)

One of the great truths that emerges from this passage, is that it's never appropriate to place an "absolute" trust in man. Not only because this can form the basis of idolatry, it's simply an enormous mistake to think anyone is infallible. The Lord is the only one who is perfect and infallible, in whom we can place our full and absolute trust without fail. *"It is better to trust in the Lord Than to put confidence in man" (Psalms 118:8).*

As we've said before, no one is perfect. Christians, though forgiven, are still only human and will undoubtedly fall short at some time or another. Even the best and most godly of leaders, teachers and pastors will make their share of mistakes.

This, however, doesn't mean that we should withhold trust entirely toward people... but only that we offer a more limited, "relative" type of trust, based on one's track record of reliability and trustworthiness. In other words, we must get to know a person's character and the history of their behavior, before we can determine how much of that limited trust we can offer.

This is one of the reasons why the scriptures tell us to get to know our pastors and spiritual leaders, so from their godly lifestyle (hopefully), we'll be able to trust their leadership. *"And we urge you, brethren, to recognize those who labor among you, and are over you in the Lord and admonish you." (1 Thessalonians 5:12).*

The Difference Between Love and Trust

Often times people in the church misunderstand the difference between the ideas of "love" and "trust." God's Word certainly teaches us to be a loving and compassionate people, however, it's possible to love and forgive persons without placing an absolute trust in them.

To illustrate this, let's say there's a school bus driver who has a drinking problem. One day while transporting a load of children, he becomes intoxicated, wrecks the bus and kills all the children. As the lone survivor of the crash, he turns to the church to seek God's forgiveness for this horrible act of irresponsibility.

So if in such a scenario, this person repents of his sin, will God forgive him? Absolutely. And should the church love and forgive this person? Of course.

And what if he would then like to volunteer to drive the church bus again for us? Do we trust him? No way! It would be unthinkable and irresponsible to put a person back in the driver's seat who has shown such recent negligence.

Certainly, we love and forgive him, but because of this man's poor track record, we could never risk the lives of passengers under his care.

Over a long period of sobriety and safe driving, this person may be able to prove that he is again capable of being trusted with a driver's license… but it would be unlikely that any authority could ever risk the safety of passengers to his supervision ever again.

We need to understand, love and forgiveness is granted unconditionally, but trust must be earned. Trust is "the acquired confidence in a person's actions or behavior… based on the evidence of a trustworthy record."

"Trust" as it applies to selecting leaders and workers in the church, should not come quickly for those who are new, especially for those who work with youth and children. This is just common sense.

And regardless of anyone's familiarity, the nature of today's amoral society makes it necessary for a church to require for all ministry workers, especially those who work with children, to first undergo a law enforcement background check before being allowed to engage in ministry. This has been standard policy in many churches for years… which we all should be thankful for. The church must be maintained as a safe environment for all, and especially for our kids.

We certainly can and should be willing to trust persons who show a reliable track-record of trustworthiness. However, it is foolish to offer any greater trust simply because a person professes to be a Christian. And to be sure, if you do so, you'll eventually get burned… and then will struggle to trust anyone.

As you might expect, the majority of professing believers are decent, honest and trustworthy people… trying to do their best to serve the Lord and walk in His ways. However there are also false believers who come into our ranks with the intent to deceive and exploit the kind, trusting, and sometimes "gullible" nature of Christian people. From my early days as a young shepherd, I learned first-hand what was involved in protecting God's flock from the threat of deceptive wolves, and while I could recount scores of incidents to illustrate this, I'll share just one that I think will make my point.

A Bitter but Valuable Lesson About Trust

Many years ago, at the conclusion of one Sunday morning's service, I extended our typical invitation for persons to come forward to receive Christ as their Savior, or to come kneel at the altar for prayer. As I did, perhaps as many as a couple dozen come forward, including a few visitors. One of these, a guy in his mid-thirties, made quite an impression when he immediately knelt and gave his heart to the Lord amid dramatic tears, sobs and pleas for the Lord's help.

Afterward, as several leaders and workers lingered to greet and encourage him in his new-found faith, "Rusty," as we came to know him, shared a startling story of tragic events that had brought him to the Lord. He explained that he and his family had been residents of a small town, a few hours away... but some weeks earlier, all three of his children had been tragically killed, and his wife critically injured, in a horrible house fire. The disaster had been further compounded by his unemployment for many previous months before this... and he had come our city, hoping to find a job and a new start for him and his wife, who was still recovering in the hospital.

Tears streamed from Rusty's face as he shared his

heartbreaking story... and all who listened wept in empathy for this devastated husband and father. It was obvious that our kind and loving folks were touched deeply, and many offered him their prayers, encouragement and anything they could do to help.

Rusty departed and we didn't see him again until the next Sunday service, but the word of his ordeal and remarkable conversion had spread quickly, and many had already reached out trying to help him. I later learned that some of our members had each given him hundreds of dollars in cash. One family even gave him a key to their home, so he could stay in a spare bedroom.

Like others, I was also touched by this man's amazing story, and was considering suggestions by members to share his need publicly to the whole church, so to raise more awareness and donations to help. However, I was also a bit concerned that our generous and loving people were listening too quickly with their hearts, without using their heads... or asking honest questions. Indeed, his story was quite unlike dozens of other flimsy scams that had come our way over the years. He was very convincing, his tears were real, we heard his sincere prayers to God... yet something seemed wrong about his story and I felt the need to do some checking.

I scheduled a time to meet with Rusty later to ask some questions, but first called the hospital in the city where his wife was recovering, only to learn that no one by that name had ever been a patient. I then called their local fire, police and town newspaper, all whom confirmed that no such fire or deaths involving children had "ever" occurred in their city or surrounding county.

Then I called a police officer in our church to run a check on his car's license plate that I had previously scribbled down. I wasn't surprised when it came back belonging to a person by a different name, a known con-artist with a criminal background, living in a nearby community just ten miles away.

Rusty wasn't able to make our scheduled meeting as planned, but he called instead... and when I answered, I confronted him with his real name, and the information that I had uncovered, asking him for an explanation. There was only silence at the other end, and finally a click when he hung up. We never saw or heard from Rusty again.

It was a bitter pill for many in our congregation to swallow, but a valuable lesson learned about trust, they would never forget. How was it possible for anyone to be so convincing and yet so deceitful, even with tears streaming at the altar, while calling on the sacred name of Jesus?

Christ put it this way, *"Not everyone who says to Me,*

'Lord, Lord,' shall enter the kingdom of heaven, but he who does the will of My Father in heaven" (Matthew 7:21).*

Increments of Trust

As I previously shared, "love and forgiveness is granted unconditionally, while trust must be earned." But let me add one more important thing. The love of Jesus in your heart, may sometimes encourage your "willingness" to trust, even before one's "track record" can be affirmed. In other words, there may be occasions that the Holy Spirit may override your normal precautions and prompt you to take small additional risks, to give someone a chance to prove himself.

"Increments of trust" are neither acts of gullibility or gambling, but when led by the Holy Spirit, become small "investments" in the growth and progress of other believers. Just like God works with all of us, first trusting us with small responsibilities, before trusting us with greater responsibilities. *"He who is faithful in what is least is faithful also in much; and he who is unjust in what is least is unjust also in much" (Luke 16:10).*

The bottom line is, under normal circumstances, you should never risk trusting anyone with anything precious, important or critical, unless they first have "proven reliability." Don't loan your car, ask them to babysit your kids, loan them a significant sum of cash, except on the basis of their proven track record.

Perhaps you can do like one Christian business owner some years ago. Having been disappointed by those who failed to pay their bill or who wrote bad checks, he displayed a sign over the counter. *"In God We Trust. All Others Pay Cash!"*

No one in the church is perfect, without an ability to fall short. So never put an infallible sense of trust in anyone but God, as He's the only one who will never fail or let you down. This will help prevent many needless potential hurts in the church.

— 6 —
Focus on Common Ground

"Now I plead with you, brethren, by the name of our Lord Jesus Christ, that you all speak the same thing, and that there be no divisions among you, but that you be perfectly joined together in the same mind and in the same judgment." (1 Corinthians 1:10)

It goes without saying, everybody has an opinion about a great many things, including the Bible, the church and so forth. However when we gather a church, a primary goal of the ministry is to bring people together around faith-building truths of the Gospel... not necessarily to explore a variety of theories or philosophies.

In other words, while any of us may have fascinating thoughts or ideas worthy of exploration, the mission of the church is not really to experiment, but rather to build consensus around principles we know to be tested and true, factual and life-changing. And we all generally get along better with our church and its leadership if we can understand and support this ministry objective.

To put this in perspective, let me cite a silly and extreme example. Let's say for instance, a dear brother comes to a church Bible study and tries to argue his theory that the

Nephilim mentioned in Genesis 6:4 are the ancient ancestors of Bigfoot creatures.

The biggest problem with this assertion is not whether such an idea is worthy of thought or discussion, but that it's out of context with what the church is trying to teach and accomplish. Not only do we not find solid scripture to substantiate such a claim, it distracts away from other more important truths that people need to hear, and could even potentially provoke quarrels or division *(Romans 1:29)*. (I've never heard of a church split over Bigfoot yet… however, I've learned to never under-estimate the divisiveness of persistent opinions!)

The church, including all believers, must continually be on guard against the "diversionary tactics" of the Devil, who is just as pleased to divert our attention away from important things, if unable to do anything more dastardly. This type of deception is especially appealing to intellectuals, who can be prone toward esoteric fascinations, curiosities and "new truth" fads, just as were the Athenians in Paul's day. *"For all the Athenians and the foreigners who were there spent their time in nothing else but either to tell or to hear some new thing" (Acts 17:21).*

To be sure, there are many interesting speculations and interpretations about things in the Bible or that pertain to spiritual things. However, the church should focus on strengthening faith toward Christ on the proven "facts" of the Gospel and of the Word of God, rather than a variety of theories and curiosities. Pressing or contending over such matters can hinder the purpose of the church, and highly opinionated people are prone to get hurt when others disagree with them, or if the leadership should ask them to tone down their opinions.

The Bible teaches for all Christians to "speak the same thing" so there can be unity in the body of Christ *(1 Corinthians 1:10)*. This is not to deny the individuality of each believer, nor to ignore the variety of personal viewpoints... but is to emphasize the need for everyone "to get on the same page"...to focus on the common ground of Jesus Christ, and to bring our words, thoughts and opinions into harmony with the Word of God, the Bible.

In other words, we need to "say what the Word says," to let God's Word speak for itself and stop trying to promote divisive opinions about it. This was essentially what the Apostle Paul was referring to, when he instructed Timothy to *"Preach the Word" (2 Timothy 4:2)*. A preacher should really only be a delivery boy of God's message, not a commentator of the message.

When I consider how the church should communicate the Gospel message, I think back to the days when the news media was required to comply with a very strict code of ethics for news reporting. They were to report only the facts accurately, without adding their speculation or commentary. However, as time has passed, the news has become less factual and more opinionated, corrupted with rumors, speculation and gossip, rather than real information. Reporters today have often evolved into manipulative commentators who try to shape what people think about the news.

Just as reporters need to get back to reporting facts, so do our preachers. Ministers of the Gospel need to stick to reporting the facts of the Good News... and they need to substantiate such truths by citing their origin from scripture. Unfortunately, today few preachers teach or quote from the Bible... and seldom cite scriptural authority for whatever they preach. Contrast this from the past powerful sermons of Evangelist Billy Graham, who was renowned for his sermons with continual references to scripture, declaring "And the Bible says."

Obviously every believer will have his or her own convictions, beliefs or speculations about a great many things, but if we continually try to thrust these things on others in the church, strife or conflict will eventually emerge... which is counterproductive for the cause of Christ.

To avoid unnecessary disappointments and hurts in the church, don't stir up division or controversies, but rather contribute toward those things that help unite the body of Christ. Avoid controversy over scriptures which are vague and foster many interpretations – stand fast upon those common, basic truths, Jesus, His life, death and resurrection – and don't add to what God's Word says.

"Every word of God is pure; He is a shield to those who put their trust in Him. Do not add to His words, lest He reprove you, and you be found a liar." (Proverbs 30:5-6)

— 7 —
Don't Expect Any Church to be Perfect

"For I know that in me (that is, in my flesh) nothing good dwells; for to will is present with me, but how to perform what is good I do not find. For the good that I will to do, I do not do; but the evil I will not to do, that I practice." (Romans 7:18-19)

These days it's quite unusual for persons of notoriety to admit their faults or weaknesses publicly. But this was precisely what Paul, the renowned apostle of the early church, divulged to the Christian body at Rome. He humbly and openly confessed that due to his sinful nature, he experienced struggles in his flesh from doing the right things. The New Living Translation describes Paul confession this way:

"I want to do what is right, but I can't. I want to do what is good, but I don't. I don't want to do what is wrong, but I do it anyway." (Romans 7:19 NLT)

So if the Apostle Paul, author of half the New Testament, admitted to such personal struggles, it should be apparent that none of us will be exempt either... nor will any church be free of flaws or shortcomings as long as they consist of imperfect creatures like us.

The fact is, **"There is no such thing as a perfect church."** There are, however, churches that do better than others, but these can sometimes be overlooked by those who don't know how to measure the true quality of a church.

Since a church refers to a body of believers, not a building, it certainly cannot be appraised accurately by the facility in which they meet. Nor can it be evaluated by whether seats are padded, how comfortable the temperature is, the convenience of the service schedule, the duration of the worship or sermon, the frequency of announcements or even how well the organization is structured or administered.

These and many other similar issues, can be obvious advantages to a church when applied appropriately, but these are only superficial matters… and have no direct correlation to how God views the church, or how well it's doing what it's supposed to. The truth of the matter is, a church might have all these and other terrific amenities and attributes, and yet still be falling short of the "spiritual" desires of God.

The kind of church that delights the Lord is the fellowship of believers who seek to love, worship and serve the Lord Jesus Christ with all their heart… and who also endeavor to love and minister to the needs of one another. It is a Bible-believing church devoted to prayer, godliness, integrity, unity, stability… and is faithful to teach and preach the truths of the Gospel and the Word of God.

It's pastor and leaders are humble Christ-like persons who strive to live what they believe and teach, and to exalt Jesus Christ in everything they say and do. Their ministry focus is to bring souls into the Kingdom of God, and to help facilitate the spiritual growth and maturity of the believers. It is a church that shows strong moral values, as well as honest and responsible stewardship in financial matters. They reject the unsavory works of the flesh, and instead demonstrate fruit of the Spirit… *"love, joy, peace, longsuffering, kindness, goodness, faithfulness, gentleness and self-control" (Galatians 5:19-23)*.

This church will seem less like a resort where perfect people hang out, and more like a spiritual hospital, where people go to get well. Instead of resenting persons with needs or imperfections, they will strive to help, comfort, love, forgive and restore lives to a right relationship with Christ. It will be evident that they care about "everyone," not just the wealthy or popular, and will always be seeking ways to get everyone involved, in order to help, give and serve with their gifts and talents.

This kind of church "may" not even have a building of their own, or offer multiple programs for every age group, or possess high tech video displays, or have the most organized, well-run operation. However, you will sense the presence of the Holy Spirit in the worship, be challenged and inspired by the preaching and teaching, and sense that you're growing closer and stronger in your relationship to Christ and God's family from each service.

Sometimes people make a comparison between a successful church and a good restaurant. But actually, the church should be less like a place you get "served" a meal, and more like a "pot-luck dinner" where everybody contributes and serves each other. What you bring with you to church is added to the content of the meal. Your contribution to the ministry and gatherings help to make it what it is.

Always remember, "a church is the combination of what its people are." So if you want your church to be the best it can be, you must be the best "you" can be. A church can never rise above what it's individual members are.

If you're not part of a church that sounds similar to our description, you should find one that does. And if your church is anything "close" to what we've described, or is at least "striving" toward such spiritual ideals, you should then be grateful to God for such a blessed fellowship.

Avoid becoming discontent or distracted over superficial issues that have nothing to do with the more substantive ideals of the church. Get involved, contribute your love, prayer, talents and resources to help make it even a better church.

Finally, imperfection is something that tends to be very subjective for those who find it. A negative person can always find fault wherever they look, while the person with a positive outlook can always find the good and beauty in almost anything.

Therefore, the most well-adjusted person in a church will generally be one who seeks out the good, encouraging and uplifting things *(Philippians 4:8)*. Persons who dwell continually on the negative, will usually find it... and will more than likely, eventually find themselves disappointed and hurt by the church.

— 8 —
Don't Seek to Promote Yourself or Your Own Agenda

"Do not lift up your horn on high; Do not speak with a stiff neck. For exaltation comes neither from the east Nor from the west nor from the south. But God is the Judge: He puts down one, And exalts another." (Psalms 75:5-7)

When seeking to assimilate into a body of believers, the best posture to assume is always one of humility and meekness, like the personality of Christ *(Matthew 11:29, Romans 12:3)*. Arrogance and pride are obnoxious traits that will always set you apart as a target for criticism, and can also invite spiritual snares that could pull you down *(Proverbs 16:18)*.

Don't promote yourself, neither campaign or strive to attain an appointed or elected position. God is the one who puts persons in such positions, and unless He does it, stay away from it... or anything that resembles politics in the church. Lift up the Lord in all that you say and all you do. Don't boast or talk about yourself. *"He who speaks from himself seeks his own glory; but He who seeks the glory of the One who sent Him is true, and no unrighteousness is in Him" (John 7:18).*

Avoid an attitude of competition, which can create friction

from unity. A competitive attitude compares self with others, and strives to rise above that comparison *(2 Corinthians 10:12)*. The philosophy of Christianity is not to try to outdo one another, but to submit to and lift up one another *(Ephesians 5:21)*. We are even told to "prefer" our brother above ourselves. *"Be kindly affectionate to one another with brotherly love, in honor giving preference to one another" (Romans 12:10)*. Light-hearted competition in games or sporting events is one thing, but strident competition between churches and Christians tends to be divisive and contrary to the faith.

Don't expect to receive preferential treatment or to get your way about everything. The Bible teaches that favoritism is wrong, and the church will try to make decisions and do things in the best interest of the whole congregation, not just a certain few. *"...but if you show partiality, you commit sin, and are convicted by the law as transgressors" (James 2:9)*.

If you do things for the church or give generous offerings, do it to bring glory to God, not to bring attention to yourself or to gain influence *(Colossians 3:17)*. The Bible even says that when you give charitable offerings, do it anonymously so to gain God's approval, not merely man's *(Matthew 6:1)*.

Avoid the trap of presuming that your opinions are always divinely inspired or are indisputable. Share your suggestions and ideas with church leaders, but don't press your opinions or personal agenda.

Sometimes, persons can feel that all their ideas come from God. They may attempt to add clout to their suggestions or complaints by saying "God told me so." Indeed, God does speak to His children, but you will not be the exclusive source through which God reveals himself in a matter. If your opinions really come from God, the Bible says that others will bear witness with it, especially His pastors and leaders *(2 Corinthians 13:1, 1 Corinthians 14:29)*. You won't even have to invoke God's name – they'll be able to tell if your ideas came from Him.

Be cautious, lest you find yourself using His name falsely, a very dangerous thing *(Exodus 20:7)*. Pastors are His representatives in His ordained chain of command, and if He wants to get something across to His church, He'll bear witness with the persons in charge.

— 9 —
Avoid Blaming the Church for Personal Problems

"You will keep him in perfect peace, whose mind is stayed on You, because he trusts in You." (Isaiah 26:3)

Many of the offenses and hurt feelings that erupt in congregational life, don't always originate there... but are often indirectly related to other issues that folks carry in with them. In other words, emotional distress experienced elsewhere can often be transferred unwittingly to other relationships and associations... such as the church.

Some refer to this as the kick-the-dog syndrome, or a tendency to lash out at others when one deals with emotional trauma, such as problems at work, marital conflict, health or financial difficulties. For obvious reasons, these and similar challenges can cause emotions to be much more sensitive and susceptible to additional conflicts and misunderstandings.

Under such circumstances, well-intended comments or actions by church folk, or from the pastor or his sermons, may be misinterpreted... or even exaggerated as deliberate offenses. And as a result, blame for continued feelings of discouragement, unhappiness or despair may be unfairly transferred or attributed to the church, its leaders or the members of the congregation.

This is one of Satan's favorite tactics, not only to prey upon the weary emotions of those struggling with such trials, but to also sow the seeds of conflict and unnecessary hurts into the body of Christ. There's nothing that the Devil desires more than to stir up wounds and strife, to separate those who are hurting, from the Lord's people who love them and want to help them.

The church must always be mindful of these tactics as we pursue our mission to be the Lord's hospital to the lost and wounded. On any given Sunday, many who gather with us may privately be dealing with unimaginable grief and heartbreak, and we must do our best to be understanding, loving and caring... both to avoid "contributing to," or becoming "a victim of" additional unnecessary offenses.

But as hard as any church and its leadership may try, people are only human... mistakes will be made, words and actions will be taken out of context, and hurts will occur. I can't tell you how many times I've regretted my own careless or poorly chosen words in the past, some that resulted in misunderstandings between persons I cared about. Yet on my worst day as a pastor, I've only had the best of intentions and never meant to wound or hurt anyone.

Consequently, "every believer" must become "their own" last line of defense against hurts and injury. This is the only way we can stop the cycle of offenses from wounding us. We can't predict what others will do or say, nor can we prevent the potential for all misunderstandings or offenses, but with God's help, we can halt them from manipulating us.

Submitting to God Will End the Blame Game

First, stop falling into the trap of blaming others for the things that the Devil inspires or exploits. Remember, "Satan" is your adversary, not flesh and blood *(Ephesians 6:12)*. This reminds me of a conflict that took place during Christ's earthly ministry, as he described His coming death and resurrection, but was sharply rebuked by Peter *(Matthew 16:21-23)*. Just imagine, Jesus was describing the most sacred and essential fact of the Gospel, His very reason and purpose, and yet his first lieutenant didn't even get it.

I think Jesus might have been a wee bit frustrated... but can you recall how He responded? He didn't reply by slamming Peter, or by calling him a blithering moron... but he said, *"Get behind Me, Satan! You are an offense to*

Me, for you are not mindful of the things of God, but the things of men!" (Matthew 16:23).

Even though Peter wasn't always the sharpest knife in the drawer, Jesus knew this foul inspiration didn't come from him. No, Peter was not demon possessed, nor was he unworthy of continued love and trust to carry on the important mission of the church, but Jesus knew that at least for those moments, Peter gave in to the impulses of his carnal mind and the seductive influence of the Devil. If this happened with one of Christ's twelve disciples, do you suppose it could happen with one of your brothers or sisters in Christ? (Duhh... of course!!!)

Secondly, the way to resist, insulate and immunize ourselves against such tactics is to submit ourselves to the Lord, and apply the strength and resources of His Holy Spirit that He provides. As James said in this passage:

"Submit yourselves therefore to God. Resist the devil, and he will flee from you. Draw nigh to God, and he will draw nigh to you." (James 4:7-8 KJV)

As I said previously, the Devil may not be the direct cause for every offense or injury that comes your way, but he certainly exploits each of them, trying to provoke and tempt your thoughts and emotions to become insulted, angry, upset, hurt at people or things. However, drawing close to the Lord and "surrendering" your "self-nature" to Him... including your heart, mind and emotions... is a sure-fire way to resist and overcome the wicked schemes of the Devil and whatever offenses may come. *(See the Armor of God Ephesians 6:10-18.)*

This of course doesn't mean that people will always behave themselves and treat you properly, or that these or other kinds of temptations or trials will stop immediately, or that the adversary will quit trying to mess with you completely. But eventually, when the Devil see's that he's unable to "push your buttons" or to "set you off" he'll flee from you... at least for a temporary "season" *(Luke 4:13).*

How Can You Submit Yourself to God?

Submitting yourself to God is obviously something that only "you" can do. It is a spiritual act of surrendering your self-willed nature to the Lordship of Jesus Christ, yielding your humble and repentant heart to the Lord, committing your ways to His. It involves a closer devotion to Jesus through prayer and His word, and a fresh new spiritual attitude in our thinking, or what Paul described as being *"renewed in the spirit of your mind," (Ephesians 4:23).*

Also, becoming immersed in worship, inspiring music, prayer, Bible teaching/preaching and the encouraging affection between fellow believers... all tends to enhance and deepen your relationship to Christ, which of course repulses and repels the Devil, while also a providing a refuge for renewed healing and joy in your heart, mind and emotions.

As we have suggested, one's mind and emotions are constant targets for the mischief and exploits of the Devil. He of course wants you to retain and dwell on the wounds and hurts of the past, so that he can continue to agitate, oppress, deceive and misguide you if he can.

But instead, walk in the renewed mind of faith, love, forgiveness and obedience to the Word of God, rather than by your old feelings or thoughts of the past... so that you will no longer be hoodwinked or oppressed by hurts or offenses. As Paul said, *"do not be conformed to this world, but be transformed by the renewing of your mind, that you may prove what is that good and acceptable and perfect will of God" (Romans 12:2).*

Finally, let your thoughts be continually renewed and filled daily with praise and thanksgiving to God, so there'll be no more accommodation for wounded or misguided thinking... so that Christ Jesus may continue to guard your heart and mind with His peace.

"Be anxious for nothing, but in everything by prayer and supplication, with thanksgiving, let your requests be made known to God; and the peace of God, which surpasses all

understanding, will guard your hearts and minds through Christ Jesus. Finally, brethren, whatever things are true, whatever things are noble, whatever things are just, whatever things are pure, whatever things are lovely, whatever things are of good report, if there is any virtue and if there is anything praiseworthy--meditate on these things" (Philippians 4:6-8).

— 10 —
Treat Others the Way You Wish to Be Treated

"Therefore, whatever you want men to do to you, do also to them, for this is the Law and the Prophets." (Matthew 7:12)

The Golden Rule taught by Jesus, was intended as a code of conduct that Christians should apply toward all people. **"Do unto others, as you would have them to do unto you."** In other words, put yourself in the other person's shoes. Give them the same consideration and courtesies that you would like offered to you. Be gracious, kind, caring and forgiving. Isn't that the way you want to be treated?

But the Golden Rule is more than a guiding regimen for our conduct, but is also a divine catalyst for other human behavior. People are "reciprocal" by nature, and tend to reflect the way they are treated. If you smile and express pleasantness, that's generally the response you can expect. If you're gracious and encouraging, people will react positively and enjoy being around you. If you offer friendliness, it will usually be offered back *(Proverbs 18:24)*.

This is the best way to interface with any group of people,

and especially the church. You'll almost always get a better reception if you engage others by expressing the attitude that you hope to receive back from them.

If, however, you make yourself a "pain" to be around, you'll soon find that many people will avoid your company. An attitude that's negative, cynical, critical, judgmental will tend to generate a similar attitude back at you. This seems to be what Jesus implied, when he said, *"Judge not, and you shall not be judged. Condemn not, and you shall not be condemned. Forgive, and you will be forgiven" (Luke 6:37).*

Many hurt feelings can be avoided if we will realize that people usually react to how we deal with them. Take self-examination of the way people might see you... by the expression on your face, your degree of friendliness, or even the way you say things.

This may sound weird, but you may need to practice smiling in mirror... so that others can interpret whether you're happy to see them. No kidding, some smiles don't look like smiles... so try it out on a friend before you scare somebody at church. No, don't fabricate yourself or be phony in any way... but just learn how to transfer what's in your heart through your face.

And if you're going to smile at people at church, be sure to make eye contact too. In the wild, if confronted by a bear, survivalists are taught to avoid eye contact. However since the person at church is not a bear, make plenty of eye contact... of course without winking, bulging or crossing your eyes. Looking away means that you're not really interested in them. Looking down means similar... or that you've lost something!

If you shake hands, be sure to offer a firm, confident two-count handshake. Take their hand firmly ("not" with a Hulk Hogan vise grip), and shake it deliberately. Take the lead, avoid the limpy, gripless technique that forces them to do all the hand shaking. And don't be hesitant or brief. That suggests you didn't want to shake their hand to begin with. And also don't forget to let go. An endless handshake is even creepier than no handshake!

And while you're smiling and shaking hands, try saying something nice, like God bless you... it's nice to meet you... wasn't the service great? (The pastor will love that one!) Offer your name, and if they respond with theirs, try to memorize it so you can greet them by name next time.

Try to avoid comments about the stench of their breath, hairy arms or body odor. (Just kidding, I'm sure you know better!) It's probably best "not" to say something like "Thanks for visiting," unless you know they really "are" a visitor... lest you find out later they've been members for decades!

People tend to gravitate toward those who are friendly, cheerful, who smile. So even if don't feel like doing these things, consider it a good exercise for your spirit, an investment toward potential friendships.

What if You Have Nothing Left to Reach Out With?

There may be times, however, that you're simply at such a low point... so discouraged, wounded or heart-broken... that you have nothing to offer anyone else. In such circumstances, there are generally loving, caring souls in the body who are seeking someone like you... to reach out to help pull you in when you need it most.

But don't wait for someone else to reach out to you. Do something... if nothing more than to simply let others know you are there. Ask for prayer, or reach out with an open heart to accept whatever efforts are made to encourage you. If you come into the church and avoid everyone, or decline to participate or isolate yourself from fellowship, it's unlikely that you'll experience the kind of love and encouragement that you need.

This reminds me of an incident during my childhood, when a stray dog was hit by a car near our rural farmhouse. When my dad discovered it lying in the ditch near death, he tried to rescue it only to get nipped and snarled at by the hurting, frightened animal.

But realizing its survival was at stake, Dad returned each day with food and water, caring for it, and calming it with his gentle words, until it finally responded with an encouraging sign of trust… the faint wag of his tail.

He was finally able to pick up the dog and brought it home where it eventually recovered. And we kept him as our loving family pet, named Buster for the remainder of his life.

Buster was like the many wounded souls that the church often reaches out to, only to get rejected and growled at. But if hurting lives want to get better, to be loved and accepted, they have to at least "wag their tail," and reach back to accept love and compassion in order for healing to begin. (I shared this illustration with a congregation once, then made the unwitting comparison, that they should all wag their tails too!)

This is an important truth that must be understood. The church can do a lot to help and to encourage, but there are things that only you can do for yourself. And unless you are willing to open yourself, to reach out to ask for or accept love and encouragement… you may become disappointed or hurt with the church. (Wag your tail!)

— 11 —
Have a Teachable and Cooperative Attitude

***"Obey those who rule over you, and be submissive, for they watch out for your souls, as those who must give account. Let them do so with joy and not with grief, for that would be unprofitable for you."
(Hebrews 13:17)***

I don't think it comes as a surprise to anyone when I say that we live in an era that is very different and foreign to the values of the past… especially as it pertains to our view of authority. Once respected as a more valued tradition in our society, rebellion toward all facets of authority became an accepted trend in the 1960's, a course that has continued to this day.

However, when we come into the church, we will find that authority is something very important that we have to rediscover and accept, starting with our submission to the "Lordship" of Jesus Christ, and extending on down the line to leaders of His Body, the church.

Accountability to authority is an essential part of Christian growth, something intended to occur within the realm of a local church, by each believer being cooperative and submissive to spiritual leaders. The Lord Jesus Christ, who is the "Head" of the church, extends His authorities through the church's pastor or elders, to provide leadership, preaching-teaching, even correction or discipline as necessary, to hold a flock accountable to the Lord's principles.

This of course, doesn't imply that church leadership has any right to exercise "absolute" or "abusive" authority. Legitimate leaders of the church are not "authoritarian," but humble, loving servants of the Lord, commissioned only to represent His interests, to speak and uphold His Word, as described by Paul's encouragement to ministers, *"Speak these things, exhort, and rebuke with all authority. Let no one despise you" (Titus 2:15). (See also 1 Timothy 5:20, 2 Timothy 3:16, 2 Timothy 4:2.)*

However, disrespect toward church leadership is a common problem today. Even mild assertions or admonitions from the pulpit are often met with defiance or scorn. Some justify their contempt, citing the imperfection and shortcomings of their leaders. However while there are specific transgressions that can invalidate one's authority to lead, being merely human is not one of them.

Keep in mind, serving in any capacity of leadership is not an easy task. Pastors and elders don't only deal with the typical challenges that come with being in charge, but they must also lead with a higher source of accountability to God, while also targeted as king-pins of Satan's attacks against the church! As much as Satan wants to destroy the lives of all Christians, his efforts against leaders are many times more intense, because he knows if he can take down a pastor or leader, he can discourage or scatter many others… and further damage the reputation of the church.

For this reason we must "never" root our faith in anyone or anyone else other than our Lord Jesus Christ (who can never fail or let us down), and we "must" also pray diligently and regularly for our pastors and leaders… as well as all secular and governmental leaders.

> *"I urge you, first of all, to pray for all people. Ask God to help them; intercede on their behalf, and give thanks for them. Pray this way for kings and all who are in authority so that we can live peaceful and quiet lives marked by godliness and dignity. This is good and pleases God our Savior" (1 Timothy 2:1-3 NLT).*

Leaders are best received by the flock by earning their respect, by serving with love, humility, transparency… seeking to apply godly counsel, wisdom and common sense to everything they do. But even when they leave much to be desired, God still recognizes them as "His" authorized representatives, whom He requires to be faithful… and holds "you" accountable to respect their God-given authority.

A good example that shows the appropriate scriptural pattern of respect toward authority, can be seen from Paul's appeal to the Jewish Council in Acts 23, when he had been falsely accused of preaching heresy against Jewish laws.

As Paul made his defense against the unjust allegation, he unknowingly challenged and insulted Ananias, the high priest, who had ordered the apostle slapped. However, when Paul realized who he was, he immediately apologized for speaking against Ananias, knowing that it's forbidden to speak against God's representative – despite the fact that Ananias' treatment of Paul was wrong.

> *"I'm sorry, brothers. I didn't realize he was the high priest," Paul replied, "for the Scriptures say, 'You must not speak evil of any of your rulers'" (Acts 23:1-5 NLT).*

This is not to ignore the fact that issues of personal offense or misunderstanding can sometimes arise between you and a leader. If that happens, it should be approached in the same biblical fashion as anyone else in the church, in the spirit of Matthew 18:15-17, Galatians 6:1, 1 Timothy 5:19. In such cases, a mature pastor or elder will generally be quick to respond with humility... and if you do likewise, more times than not it will lead to peace, forgiveness and reconciliation.

Of course there's also the possibility you may come to a place that you cannot fully support the views, doctrines or practices of a particular church or its leaders. This is best determined by first sitting down with those in authority, discussing and asking questions, before simply looking for another church. Some people make it a bad habit of developing opinions based on assumptions, rumors, or by how things "seem" to be.

Christians should be people who seek out truth, and find out the facts, before making conclusions about anything. *"Do not judge according to appearance, but judge with righteous judgment" (John 7:24). (See Deuteronomy 13:14, 19:18)*

But to challenge, contend with or join a revolt against the authorities of the church is never a good idea. It will only hinder your spiritual progress, and can even possibly alienate you from a right relationship with the Lord. When a church needs changes in leadership, it must come from the Lord... through the prayerful consideration of a board, congregational referendum, or sanctioned authorities to whom the leaders are accountable.

Consequently, when becoming part of a particular church, you'll get along much better if you come to terms with whomever is in charge, and offer them your cooperation, respect, and a teachable spirit. If you retain a rigid, inflexible or defiant attitude in whatever church you become part of, you will probably get hurt.

— 12 —
Don't Oppose or Hinder the Church

"These six things the LORD hates, yes, seven are an abomination to Him: A proud look, a lying tongue, hands that shed innocent blood, a heart that devises wicked plans, feet that are swift in running to evil, a false witness who speaks lies, and one who sows discord among brethren." (Proverbs 6:16-19)

Something that the Lord, especially dislikes, is the promotion of discord, division or strife in the body of Christ. This is because Satan can use such diversions to damage the spiritual stability of believers… or hinder souls from coming into the church and being saved.

In fact, one of the most stern warnings Jesus ever uttered, was against those who might cause any of His followers to falter in their faith:

> *"But whoever causes one of these little ones who believe in Me to stumble, it would be better for him if a millstone were hung around his neck, and he were thrown into the sea." (Mark 9:42)*

What everyone should understand is that the church belongs to our Lord Jesus Christ *(Matthew 16:18)*. He considers it to be a part of himself, His body *(1 Corinthians 12:20),* and also considers any offense against it, as an attack against Himself... just as He did when Saul persecuted and killed Christians, prior to his conversion *(Acts 9:4-5).*

We should never find ourselves in a situation that we are opposing, attacking or contributing to hindrances or problems in the church in any way. That goes for the individual brothers and sisters, as well as the organization, ministries and missions.

Keep in mind, this is not to suggest that there aren't occasions that a ministry needs honest, constructive criticism. Note the word "constructive." Finding fault or complaining is easy... but what a church really needs are thoughtful, helpful suggestions to bring solutions... and "your" willingness to roll up your sleeves to help if necessary.

Every church and pastor needs the honest feedback of the congregation, and all believers need to feel that their thoughts, concerns or suggestions are taken seriously. Leaders are wise to welcome this kind of openness, which can be quite helpful and may in fact help "preempt" or diffuse the possibility of festering problems or discontent.

Obviously, there are also situations that a church or its leaders may need correction, or to be held responsible for unbiblical actions or behavior. This kind of thing, however, can't come by hostile attacks against the church or its leaders... but must come only from the sanctioned authorities within the defined governing framework, such as denominational leaders, a board of elders, pastors, deacons, or by congregational referendum, etc. And must always approached with love, humility and with the intent to correct, restore or reconcile, in the spirit of Matthew 18:15-17, Galatians 6:1, and 1 Timothy 5:19.

It does not help, nor does it serve the righteousness of God, to snipe at, disparage, spread rumors against, or stir up turmoil in the church... and doing so can put you on opposing sides against the Lord and His church. The church belong to the Lord Jesus, and He reserves the right to hold it accountable within His own measurement of judgment and patience.

If you're displeased with the church in some way, go to your knees and pray for it and its leaders... be forthright to share your concerns with the pastor or elders, and offer your suggestions and willingness to help make improvements... OR as a last resort, prayerfully seek out another church that better suites you or your needs. But "never" become a source of agitation or hindrance to the church.

By all means, avoid seeking secular litigation against a church or other Christians at all costs, and only if all other scriptural remedies fail, such as Christian arbitration conducted within the framework of Matthew 18:15-17.

Read carefully this very strong admonition from the Apostle Paul, which I cite from the New Living Translation for the sake of clarity:

> *"When one of you has a dispute with another believer, how dare you file a lawsuit and ask a secular court to decide the matter instead of taking it to other believers! Don't you realize that someday we believers will judge the world? And since you are going to judge the world, can't you decide even these little things among yourselves? Don't you realize that we will judge angels? So you should surely be able to resolve ordinary disputes in this life. If you have legal disputes about such matters, why go to outside judges who are not respected by the church? I am saying this to shame you. Isn't there anyone in all the church who is wise enough to decide these issues? But instead, one believer sues another—right in front of unbelievers! Even to have such lawsuits with one another is a defeat for you. Why not just accept the injustice and leave it at that? Why not let yourselves be cheated? Instead, you yourselves are the ones who do wrong and cheat even your fellow believers" (1 Corinthians 6:1-8 NLT).*

Paul leaves little room for confusion as to how we should view secular lawsuits between Christians. Remember that Jesus said that the world is watching, and will know that we are His disciples by our love for one another. (Now doesn't that put a wet blanket on lawsuit plans between believers?)

Neither is it a good idea to oppose or badmouth God's duly authorized pastor or leader, such as seen in the case of Paul's challenge to Ananias in Acts 23. As we've already suggested in our previous chapter, church pastors and leaders are not without their need for accountability, which may require correction or discipline as well.

However, to repeat again, "this must come from the Lord, through those who are His sanctioned authorities." And just like when dealing with all God's people, it must be administered with love, humility and the intent to correct, restore or reconcile, in the spirit of Matthew 18:15-17, Galatians 6:1, and 1 Timothy 5:19.

The Word of God considers it a serious matter to "touch" God's anointed – either with our hostile words or our actions. Imperfect as they may sometimes be, they are "His" representatives. Review carefully the following passage:

> **"He permitted no one to do them wrong; Yes, He reproved kings for their sakes, Saying, Do not**

touch My anointed ones, And do My prophets no harm." (Psalms 105:14-15)

You may recall the story of when David spared the life of King Saul, during the time that the king and his army were hunting to kill David in the wilderness of Ein Gedi. David was able to sneak up on Saul in a cave, but instead of killing him as his men urged, he only cut off a corner of his robe... to prove later that he had, but declined the opportunity to slay him.

But David was later troubled by this small gesture... citing that he knew it was improper to even touch the Lord's anointed leader. *"...it happened afterward that David's heart troubled him because he had cut Saul's robe. And he said to his men, The Lord forbid that I should do this thing to my master, the Lord's anointed, to stretch out my hand against him, seeing he is the anointed of the Lord"* (1 Samuel 24:5-6).

As far as David was concerned, the Lord chose Saul, and his fate should be left to God's judgment, not his own. *"Let the Lord judge between you and me, and let the Lord avenge me on you. But my hand shall not be against you"* (1 Samuel 24:12).

This doesn't mean that any minister should be allowed to get away with trespasses or sinful deeds... only that he must be dealt with scripturally, and with respect to his role as the Lord's representative.

If a minister has done wrong against you in some way, don't incriminate yourself by responding in an unbiblical manner – don't lash out against him with rumors, or run him down behind his back.

You should go and confront him privately according to the scriptural fashion described in Matthew 18:15-17. If the first and second attempts do not bring a resolution, take the matter to the spiritual body to which he is accountable, such as the church board, or denominational overseers – any correction or discipline should be left to them.

Keep in mind, an accusation against a minister is a serious matter and should not be accepted unless it can be substantiated by other witnesses. *"Do not receive an accusation against an elder except from two or three witnesses"* (1 Timothy 5:19).

And what if your minister or pastor has no authority to whom he is accountable? Then you'll need to ask yourself why you're in that particular church. Any minister serving in a role of spiritual leadership, must obviously be accountable to the Lord… but also to the Lord's sanctioned authorities, such as a board, denomination, or council of other ministers or advisors. Leaders are only human and an absence of accountability creates too many potential risks and temptations.

When things are not as they should be in the church or

with its leadership, there are honorable and scriptural ways to help promote improvements or resolve inequities. However, it's unethical to oppose the church or attack its leadership, and persons who do so will likely end up hurt, bitter or possibly worse.

— 13 —
Be Committed to Forthrightness and Truth

"Moreover if your brother sins against you, go and tell him his fault between you and him alone. If he hears you, you have gained your brother. But if he will not hear you, take with you one or two more, that by the mouth of two or three witnesses every word may be established. And if he refuses to hear them, tell it to the church. But if he refuses even to hear the church, let him be to you like a heathen and a tax collector." (Matthew 18:15-17)

Conflict resolution is a very important matter in the body of Christ. If a fellow believer wrongs you (*"hamartano," ἁμαρτάνω, to "sin or trespass" against you*) in some significant way, Jesus teaches you to go and confront your brother privately in an attempt to resolve your differences. Among other reasons, this is because the Lord wants peace to prevail in His church.... and He wants believers to be honest and forthright with each other, so that truth has a healthy environment in which to flourish. *"Confess your trespasses to one another, and pray for one another, that you may be healed..." (James 5:16).*

Hiding or absorbing significant offenses is not only a sure way to suppress the openness and humility that's needed in the body of Christ, but harbored wounds can also lead to bitterness which can damage your personal relationship with God.

Being prompt to confront an offender is not only the best way to avoid an impediment to your spiritual health, but most offenses in the church result from simple misunderstandings, and many could be quickly resolved if the offended parties would just go to the source and find out the facts.

Unfortunately, some offended people will just absorb the offense silently, while growing increasingly resentful. Whenever possible, we should strive to "nip things in the bud," not to drag our feet from seeking a resolution. *"Do not let the sun go down on your wrath," (Ephesians 4:26).*

Satan routinely seeks to exploit such unresolved offenses or disputes as a method to sow discontent or strife. Therefore, it is important to God, and a matter of obedience to His Word, that such matters are confronted promptly and scripturally.

Reasons to Confront Our Offenders:

(1) To maintain peace in the body of Christ *(Ephesians 4:1-3).* Whenever there is friction and turmoil in the body, it distracts others from their spiritual progress and from receiving from God's Word. It creates an uninviting atmosphere for the church, hinders souls from coming to Christ, and can even grieve the Holy Spirit *(Ephesians 4:30-32)*.

(2) So Satan cannot gain advantage over us *(2 Corinthians 2:10-11)*. For our own spiritual well-being, we must be quick to resolve our differences between our brethren and forgive. Satan can hinder one's spiritual life, even deceiving them into walking away from the church or from the Lord, through harbored bitterness or unforgiveness *(Matthew 18:35)*.

(3) To restore a fallen brother *(Galatians 6:1)*. Christians must make every attempt to restore a brother or sister who has fallen into sin. Our love for our brother's spiritual well-being requires us to confront his transgression against us, so that he might repent and be reconciled to God.

(4) To "gain" or reconcile with our brother *(Matthew 18:15b)*. Every family knows what it is to have occasional spats or differences, but ultimately offenders must apologize when they're wrong, and we must be willing to make-up, reconcile and forgive, so that our relationships can be restored and not impaired.

(5) So that an offender who has perpetrated sin, might be held accountable from repeating similar offenses *(Luke 17:3)*. Another important purpose in confronting our offender, or if necessary "taking one or two others" or by "telling the church" *(Matthew 18-15-17)*, is for the well-being of the church and all parties involved. Our attitude must not be to seek retribution for our offense, but to hold the transgressor accountable for his actions, so this pattern will not be repeated, either by this offender or by others who see no consequences to similar behavior.

Obviously, not all offenses or hurt feelings will be the result of what we might think of as a sin or trespass, nor will always rise to the level of this type of intervention. Yet the "spirit" of what Jesus taught was to always be open and honest with each other, to seek ways to resolve our differences. His desire is for the body of Christ to avoid rancor, animosity, strife... and to be united in forgiveness, peace, and love for each other.

First, Go to Your Brother Privately *(Matthew 18:15)*

Jesus said for you to first go to the offending party, confront them with the offense, and keep the matter private between yourselves. Remember, the objective is not merely to seek amends for how you were violated, but to seek "reconciliation" between your brother, and his restoration to a right relationship with God.

Your attitude is very important. While Jesus taught that it was appropriate to "rebuke" your brother if he sins against you (Luke 17:3-4), this doesn't mean to assault him with anger and provocation. Doing so is likely to make matters worse. By all means, seek the Lord for His strength to take the "high road," so that you confront your offender with grace and humility. Your motive is not reprisal for the hurt, but to invite repentance... offering forgiveness, with the hope to restore your fellowship.

Why is the matter to be first kept private between you two? Because your love for your brother requires it. If we are sincerely committed to love for the brethren as Jesus commands *(John 13:34)*, then even if a brother has sinned against us or has done us wrong, we would not want to hinder his restoration by damaging his reputation within the body. If this person's transgression against you is circulated within the body, but later he repents, many in the body will have already judged this brother and the accusations will have damaged their opinion of him. By spreading our accusation against an offending party, it builds a consensus against them and makes it difficult, if not nearly impossible, to restore that person to the body should they repent and desire to make things right.

Also, we need to first investigate the facts and find out for sure whether a trespass has really occurred. This is another reason why you are to first go privately to the brother in question – to confront him with the alleged offense and hear his side of the story. If we disclose the offense to friends in the body, we may later discover that the matter was only a misunderstanding. But by then, their reputation will have been damaged by our allegations.

Many people foolishly allow themselves to become offended by misinterpreting other's intentions, or listening to rumors and second-hand information which always contain distortions or exaggerations. Many offenses could be settled easily by simply confronting the offending party and hearing their explanation. You'd be surprised how many people don't even bother to investigate the facts or hear the other side of the story. Don't ever forget, "There's always two sides to a story!" Never assume you know the truth of a matter until you've heard all sides! (Just ask your spouse!)

Of course, there would also be far fewer misunderstandings in the body of Christ, if people would be firmly devoted to love for their brethren. Love for the brethren gives us a desire to believe the best in our brother. Love gives them the "benefit of the doubt," instead of jumping to conclusions and always expecting the worst. The Living Bible says *"If you love someone... you will always believe in him, always expect the best of him" (1 Corinthians 13:7 TLB)*.

If the trespass is proven valid, and the offender repents for their misdeed, you are to express your forgiveness *(Luke 17:3-4)*. Let the matter be forever ended, and carry no resentment toward them. Remember, if they repent, but you continue to harbor bitterness, you too become a perpetrator of sin *(Matthew 6:14-15, Acts 8:23, Ephesians 4:31-32)*.

Second, Take Another Brother *(Matthew 18:16)*

If your private attempt fails to resolve the issue, you are then to take one or two other Christians and again, confront the offending party. The presence of another Christian is as a witness to strengthen the serious effect of confrontation, to collaborate the exhortation of scripture, to amplify the Lord's presence in the meeting, and to verify the exchange of testimony.

Third, Tell Church Leadership *(Matthew 18:17)*

If the first and second attempts fail, Jesus said then to "tell it to the church." This doesn't mean stand up and tell the "entire" church body, as this could cause further conflict in the fellowship, confuse visitors, or injure the faith of young believers. (Not to mention, it might also give your pastor a seizure!) The meaning is that the church pastors or elders should be told, so then to become involved in dealing with the offending party.

Finally, only after these three prescribed attempts fail, we are no longer required to entreat them with the same courtesies shown to other brethren. According to Jesus, they may be dealt with in the same fashion as we would a heathen or publican.

What to Do if "You" Trespass

If you are aware of sins or trespasses you have committed against your brother, you have a responsibility to go to him and seek his forgiveness. Should you not attempt reconciliation, this will hinder your relationship with God. Your worship, your prayers and service to the Lord will not be acceptable. *"Therefore if you bring your gift to the altar, and there remember that your brother has something against you, leave your gift there before the altar, and go your way. First be reconciled to your brother, and then come and offer your gift" (Matthew 5:23-24).*

Note that the scripture says "if your 'brother' has something against you." In other words, you might not agree that you have legitimately violated your brother – or you may have done so inadvertently. But if you are aware that "they" harbor an offense against you, you still are obligated to go and try to resolve the issue. Be willing to be humble and submissive to others, even if you don't feel you're at fault. "You can either be right about everything, or you can have friends... but you usually can't have both."

Try to understand your brother's point of view. Don't be so rigid and self-righteous that you stand in the way of a brother's reconciliation with you or with God *(Romans 15:1-3)*.

Offer your sincere (not pretentious) apology for any offense, whether intentional or not, and make every effort to reconcile so that your relationship with God will not be hindered. Whether or not they pardon you, you have done your part and released your soul from blame.

Finally, it's not really possible to have a relationship with any group of people without occasional misunderstandings and offenses. And unless you commit yourself to confront these issues in the way Jesus described, it is very likely you will become hurt in the church.

— 14 —
Be Devoted to Love and Forgiveness

"He who loves his brother abides in the light, and there is no cause for stumbling in him." (1 John 2:10)

We've already touched on this in previous chapters, but this is a subject that we cannot emphasize enough. Christians will avoid a lot of problems if they will just commit themselves to an unconditional love for their brethren. The practice of loving and forgiving the brethren – all the brethren, not just the lovable ones – helps to keep us from stumbling. As Paul wrote, *"...walk in love, as Christ also has loved us and given Himself for us..." (Ephesians 5:2)*.

Unforgiveness is among the Devil's favorite ploys to use against believers. Satan knows that if he can keep poking at you with offenses and wounds... he can possibly manipulate you into harboring resentment, anger, bitterness or grudges toward your fellow believers, and cause you to stumble in your relationship with God, as this scripture says:

"...look diligently lest anyone fall short of the grace of God; lest any root of bitterness

springing up cause trouble, and by this many become defiled" (Hebrews 12:15).

For this reason, the Apostle Paul warns that it actually brings a heaviness or sorrow to the Holy Spirit when believers will not forgive and love one another. He said, *"And do not grieve the Holy Spirit of God, by whom you were sealed for the day of redemption. Let all bitterness, wrath, anger, clamor, and evil speaking be put away from you, with all malice. And be kind to one another, tenderhearted, forgiving one another, just as God in Christ also forgave you" (Ephesians 4:30-32).*

Is it really possible to lose one's redemption by merely holding a grudge against someone? Jesus seemed to leave no room for doubt on the subject. He clearly stated that God's forgiveness is conditional, on the basis of "your" forgiveness... that His forgiveness is not possible if you choose to withhold forgiveness toward others. Look carefully at what Jesus said:

"For if you forgive men their trespasses, your heavenly Father will also forgive you. But if you do not forgive men their trespasses, neither will your Father forgive your trespasses" (Matthew 6:14-15).

Is it then, no wonder why Satan works so hard to stir up turmoil, and tries to keep you from forgiving and loving each other? If he can trick you into harboring bitterness, he knows that you will distance yourself from God's forgiveness, and you could ultimately end up in the lake of fire *(Revelation 20:15)*. The consequences of unforgiveness are serious and devastating, and is reiterated in many scriptures, such as Matthew 18:21-35, Mark 11:25-26, Matthew 6:12, Luke 6:37, Luke 11:4.

Indeed, there's probably nothing else that has been more destructive to the body of Christ than unforgiveness. It has split churches, destroyed families, and ruined lives. And the Bible makes it clear that the person who withholds forgiveness, resides in an "unforgiven" state with God.

Their prayers go unanswered, they lack the Lord's joy and peace… and will often struggle with a critical and judgmental attitude, along with a dissatisfaction with the people and circumstances around them. They may blame their unhappiness on a variety of things, but the real problem lies with the fact that they're not in a right relationship with the Lord.

Therefore, it's important to be aware of Satan's strategy, and to arm yourself with unconditional love and forgiveness. As Paul said in the following verse:

> ***"A further reason for forgiveness is to keep from being outsmarted by Satan; for we know what he is trying to do." (2 Corinthians 2:11 TLB)***

What is Satan trying to do? He wants to help you bury and conceal your offenses so deep down in your soul, that its roots are unable to be plucked out easily. The longer you wait to forgive, the more entrenched the resentment can become... which will eventually bring spiritual damage and distance you from your relationship with God. As the Living Bible helps clarify, *"Watch out that no bitterness takes root among you, for as it springs up it causes deep trouble, hurting many in their spiritual lives" (Hebrews 12:15 TLB).*

As we have said, Jesus taught that loving God and loving one another were the highest ideals of His followers *(Luke 10:27)*. Love and forgiveness is the most basic standard of Christianity – it is the mark of followers of Christ – the highest display of spiritual maturity. Love is the evidence that you are a true follower of Jesus Christ. *"We know that we have passed from death to life, because we love the brethren" (1 John 3:14).*

Therefore, every Christian can be protected and immunized from the damaging effects by applying and obeying this simple scripture:

"Make allowance for each other's faults, and forgive anyone who offends you. Remember, the Lord forgave you, so you must forgive others.

*Above all, clothe yourselves with love, which binds us all together in perfect harmony."
(Colossians 3:13-14 NLT)*

— 15 —
Don't Get Caught up in the Offenses of Others

"Lord, who may abide in Your tabernacle? Who may dwell in Your holy hill? He who walks uprightly, And works righteousness, And speaks the truth in his heart; He who does not backbite with his tongue, Nor does evil to his neighbor, Nor does he take up a reproach against his friend." (Psalms 15:1-3)

One of the great characteristics of the body of Christ is to care about the burdens and sufferings of one another. However, as we seek to console and encourage friends who have been offended or wounded, our compassion and empathy may sometimes tempt us to take up their offense, or take their part against whomever they blame for their injury… such as another brother, the church, or even the pastor.

First please be forewarned, to adopt the offense of someone else is always an unwise thing to do, as expressed in this helpful and amusing passage from Proverbs: *"Interfering in someone else's argument is as foolish as yanking a dog's ears" (Proverbs 26:17 NLT)*.

For one thing, your friend might be the cause of his own offense. His hurt feelings may be due to a misunderstanding, a difference of opinion… perhaps a result of his own immature attitude, or even emotional instability. There are always two sides to a story, and no one should ever develop an opinion based on one side, or without knowing all the facts.

But even before considering any facts, you should steer clear of taking sides and lovingly advise your offended friend to follow the specific guidance provided by Jesus, as we addressed previously, from Matthew 18. *"If another believer sins against you, go privately and point out the offense. If the other person listens and confesses it, you have won that person back." (Matthew 18:15 NLT).*

Whenever persons are offended by another in the body of Christ, the first person to be notified about it, should be the one who did the offending. Sometimes an offender doesn't even know he's done anything wrong, until you bring it to his attention. As Jesus said, *"go privately and point out the offense,"* before proceeding to the next steps of taking witnesses, or telling the church if necessary *(Matthew 18:15-17)*.

The matter is to be kept private just between you two in this first instance, because not only is it no one else's business, but many offenses are the products of simple misunderstandings, that can be often be clarified and reconciled when confronted directly and privately. *"When arguing with your neighbor, don't betray another person's secret" (Proverbs 25:9 NLT).*

However, if the offended person first runs to their friends, and spills their hurts, anger and bruised emotions to those who will listen... this makes a simple reconciliation between two parties difficult to achieve... especially after one-sided rumors, gossip or hearsay is spread to other members of the body, who may begin to take sides.

Obviously, for this reason the scriptures warn us from taking sides, as this passage suggests:

"My dear friends, as a follower of our Lord Jesus Christ, I beg you to get along with each other. Don't take sides. Always try to agree in what you think" (1 Corinthians 1:10 CEV).

In many cases, offended persons don't intend to spread their grievances or to cause turmoil in the church, but all too often, such individuals allow their emotions of hurt, fear, anger, pride to dissuade them from "confronting" their offender (as Jesus instructed), which only allows the unresolved issue to fester and grow worse. And of course, the matter will then begin to circulate through the cycle of rumors and whisperings, as the offended party confides in and seeks the support of trusted friends.

In other cases, some people struggle with a life-long habit, that that seeks to wedge or pit friends against those whom they think have offended them, or who pose a threat to their emotions. Similar to a child who runs to his mother to take his part, when his dad is trying to correct or discipline him in some way.

Regardless, the epidemic of "taking sides" in disputes or offenses can pose real and legitimate hindrances to our spiritual well-being, as well as the harmony of any fellowship… and as believers in the Lord Jesus Christ, we all need to get on the same page, and come into scriptural agreement how such matters should be handled. Every believer should know and understand the Biblical method of conflict resolution, as outlined by Jesus in Matthew 18:15-17.

We should be determined and willing to be open and forthright with each other, to love and forgive, to prevent wedges from developing between us, and to promote peace, fellowship and unity in the body of Christ.

We must repent of the old divisive ways of the world, and stick with the scriptural methods of dealing with these issues. Otherwise division and strife can take on a life of its own, which Satan can exploit to promote further injury, causing splits in the body, or even driving people away from their faith and relationship with Christ… which only adds to the hurts and wounds of our loving Savior who suffered and gave His life for the church.

When these kinds of things happen in a fellowship, and

assuredly they will at some time or another, take special precaution to guard your heart, as this is one of the most common pitfalls that can occur in the church. Never take sides, except for the truth and righteousness of our Lord Jesus and His word.

You certainly should always love and encourage an offended friend, but ALWAYS point them to the Biblical method of resolving their disputes in Matthew 18:15-17, and reserve forming opinions or taking sides, lest you find yourself a partaker in another person's sins... or lest you also become offended and hurt with the church.

— 16 —
Don't Personalize Everything That's Preached

"He who has ears to hear, let him hear!" (Matthew 13:9)

Obviously, every pastor preaches with the hope that everyone will take his message personally and apply it to his or her own life. When listening to a sermon, we should always open our heart to hear whatever the Lord might be saying to us… and "if the shoe fits, wear it." (A cliché that began back when people still wore shoes!)

Sometimes, however, the sermon may not fit us "precisely." While we all should glean a general benefit and application from whatever sermon we hear, not every message will apply specifically to our life or situation at that moment… and the "shoe" may sometimes fit someone else more precisely than ourselves.

But even though a congregational sermon is generally intended for a broad range of people, there are occasions that persons may think the preacher is subtly pointing his sermon directly at them… which can obviously cause individuals to feel offended.

I especially recall one fellow from a congregation years ago, who sometimes felt singled out and would get up and stomp out of the service. He would return later after thinking things through, but no such attempts were being made to preach directly at him, and this was just an unnecessary distraction for both him and the church.

A pastor generally won't deliberately single persons out in his sermons for a variety of reasons, but perhaps the most obvious is that he simply has too many other people and matters to consider during the limited time-frame of his sermons. His focus must be on what the Lord wants to say through him to the broad group of people in attendance.

Besides this, the pastor knows that targeting anyone in his message would be unacceptable to most people. Any minister realizes that such tactics are not only unproductive... but may even result in a dwindling or disgruntled congregation. (A pastor should always be concerned if a crowd asks to meet with him, while carrying torches and pitchforks!)

One misunderstanding that contributes to this, is that people sometimes feel their pastor can focus on them, the same way they can focus on him and his ministry. When he stands in front of the congregation week after week, folks come to know him more personally than he is able to know them, and they occasionally develop the illusion that the pastor dwells upon or remembers their personal details in the same way they remember his. This can lead them to a presumption that he focuses on them, their personal details or problems when he preaches.

When persons feel targeted this way, there may be a variety of reasons. They might (1) be under conviction about a particular matter, (2) be especially self-conscious, (3) have been dealing with emotional distress, (4) have spent time counseling with the pastor, or (5) have been previously corrected or offended by the pastor in some way.

But the most likely scenario is that the Holy Spirit is involved, using the random words of the sermon, scriptures or metaphors to speak more specifically to the hearts of those whom He's already been convicting or dealing with about various matters *(John 16:8)*. Even though a minister prays to be led and directed by the Lord in the things he preaches, he is usually unaware that his preaching has any more significance for one person than another.

If you feel targeted by the preaching of the pastor, the wisest thing to do is to first consider the possibility that God might be trying to personally communicate some things to you. Seek the Lord and His word, ask Him for His guidance and counsel, and make sure your heart is in a right relationship with Him. Usually the things that His Spirit deals with us about in this fashion, won't come as a complete surprise... but will probably confirm matters that you were already aware of.

If however, you can't find a connection to what the Holy Spirit might be trying to say to you, but still continue to feel targeted (that is, if the pastor is in a position to know details about your life or situation), then simply go to him in the spirit of Matthew 18, and ask him if he's trying to tell you something.

Any minister who's been truly trying to communicate something subtly, would never pass up your invitation to confide it plainly to your face. And if he can't offer anything, nor has a clue as to what you're talking about, then you should probably just forget about it.

Sometimes the Lord may lead a pastor to unknowingly make comments or choose words that have special significance to you... perhaps with the intent of getting your attention. And if not careful to be led by the Holy Spirit, the Devil can also inspire or exploit careless words in an attempt to cause harm.

But then again, pastors can also say things for no particular reason at all, except that they get their foot caught in their mouth, like what occurred to me once in the past while visiting a congregation as a guest speaker.

That Sunday morning I was speaking on what the Bible says about the "reprobate mind," and made several comments about how persistent rebellion and sin against God could affect one's mental state. And for whatever reason, I made a number of lighthearted remarks, something like, *"It can actually drive you nuts!"* and *"You might go bananas!"* The congregation at large didn't seem especially amused, but a half-dozen middle-aged men sitting together near the front, seemed to appreciate my quips... and were grinning and chuckling.

Afterward, as I greeted and shook hands with those departing at the door, I was pleased to see these same gentlemen, who before leaving expressed how much they enjoyed the service.

"Nice fellas," I said to the pastor standing nearby. *"Are they brothers, or relatives... why did they all come to church together?"* I asked.

The pastor just looked at me with a grin, and said simply, *"We bus these guys in from the hospital every Sunday, so they can worship with us,"* he said. *"Oh yeah? What hospital is that?"* I asked. *"The state mental hospital,"* he replied.

Oops! Of course, I had no idea... and was stunned that I had uttered such thoughtless remarks that could have been misconstrued as ridicule or making fun of them. But amazingly none of these good-natured guys seemed especially sensitive or offended in any way.

Obviously my flippant comments were made with only good intentions, and if the enemy inspired them or was attempting to exploit careless words to cause injury, it at least didn't work. Ironically, these guys seemed to be the only ones entertained by my wisecracks... which helped me to better understand the type of audience that best relates to my sense of humor!

Sometimes we try to make sense out of senseless things that happen. Pastors are simply human, will make plenty of mistakes, and can sometimes unintentionally say or do goofy things. But please don't presume that their intent is to target you or to cause you harm... lest you find yourself offended and hurt with the church.

— 17 —
How to Recover from Hurts You've Experienced

By the time you reach this point in the book, it's my hope that you may be starting to see the ministry of the church a fresh new light. While I composed this writing mainly to prepare believers and help "preempt" hurts before they happen, there's a likelihood that many will read this because of wounds they've already experienced. And if you're one of the many casualties I've described, I pray that the Lord can use the truths shared here to begin a recovery process in your heart.

Don't Run, but Face Your Hurts

First, for the sake of your recovery, I urge you... please don't run away from your wounds, but face and deal with them. The premise of what Jesus taught about resolving conflicts in Matthew 18:15-17, is based on the idea of standing your ground, confronting those in a Christ-like fashion who have done you wrong, and bringing the matter to a resolution.

Yes, this is more challenging than choosing the easy way out, to simply quit or run away. But be assured that if you do decide to run, you will face the same thing over and over again in your life... and you will never fully recover from the accumulation of repeated wounds.

Just think of it... if Satan realizes that he can cause you to give up and run so easily... what kind of manipulation and control does that give him over you? He clearly will be enabled to cause all kinds of havoc in your life... your marriage, your career, your relationships, etc. And obviously, you may drift from one church to another... or eventually to none at all, to escape the wounds that constantly keep hounding you.

So if you've been offended by persons in your church, should you just quit and find another one? No, my advice to you is to first apply the guidelines of Matthew 18:15-17, and follow it through to a resolution. The only way you can truly heal and fully recover from a wound is to confront it with the antiseptic of truth, and bandage it with the protection of love and forgiveness. Seeking a biblical resolution is the best remedy for you, the offender and for the church.

If after seeking to resolve such matters, you still feel inclined to worship elsewhere, it may be possible that the Lord is leading you toward such a move. However, be cautious from making impulsive decisions. Pray and seek the counsel of God's Word, and if possible, go speak with and pray with your pastor or other church leaders. No shepherd ever wants to lose a valued member of his flock, but most pastors I know, only want what's best for you and your family. If the Lord is leading you on, let it be with your pastor's love and blessings.

Forgiveness Paves the Road to Recovery

If someone trespassed against you as outlined in Matthew 18:15-17, you'll want to get started by following the Lord's guidelines that we previously addressed in chapter 13. But before that, first come before the presence of our Lord Jesus, to seek His help. Without inviting Him and His involvement, there's little progress that any of us can ever make in our lives as believers. *"He who abides in Me, and I in him, bears much fruit; for without Me you can do nothing" (John 15:5).* Ask Jesus to give you the strength to seek a resolution with love and grace, and the willingness to relinquish whatever resentments or hostilities you may feel toward those whom Satan has used to hurt you.

As I've already shared, not all offenses or hurt feelings may be the result of something that requires this kind of intervention. However the general theme of what Jesus taught about resolving conflict remains valid. He wants his followers to have an attitude of honesty and reconciliation toward each other, to resolve conflicts and work out our differences with humility, repentance and forgiveness.

Fortunately, good results are frequent when we seek to resolve our offenses scripturally... and especially when we attempt to do so with a humble and gracious attitude. It's a wonderful thing when an offender can admit their errors and sincerely repents. I personally have never found it difficult to forgive anyone who has apologized and asked for forgiveness. (I'm grateful for parents who were loving and forgiving, and likewise passed these traits on to their children.)

But regardless of the outcome, even if an apology does not come, you still have no other choice but to forgive your offender and move on with your life in Christ. Why? Because unforgiveness is an enemy of your soul, a tool of the Devil to bring you down and destroy you. And sadly, I've known many believers who have allowed this very thing... whose unforgiven grievances became a cancer of bitterness that consumed them.

Remember the conditional nature of the Lord's forgiveness for your sins. Jesus said, *"For if you forgive men their trespasses, your heavenly Father will also forgive you. But if you do not forgive men their trespasses, neither will your Father forgive your trespasses"* (Matthew 6:14-15). His deal is, He will forgive you, but you must forgive others. Or as the late C.S. Lewis wrote decades ago, *"To be a Christian means to forgive the inexcusable because God has forgiven the inexcusable in you."*

An Extraordinary Model of Forgiveness

I understand how difficult it can be to forgive in some

instances of extreme offense and hurt. However, think about the testimonies of others who have endured even greater injuries and injustice, and yet found a way to forgive.

Such was the case of 32-year-old Michelle Knight, who found the grace to forgive the man who held her captive and abused her in the basement of his Cleveland home for eleven years. Knight was kidnapped in 2001, and for more than a decade, she and two other abducted women, Amanda Berry and Gina DeJesus, were kept bound with chains and continuously raped and beaten by this monster, until their escape in 2013. After their abductor was captured and sentenced to life in prison, he committed suicide shortly thereafter in his cell.

Knight eventually recounted the details of her years of torture, during which she became pregnant five times, and was beaten and starved until she miscarried each child. During her weekly rapes, she was forced to wear a motorcycle helmet with a face mask so no one could hear her screams. She was beaten so severely, it left her with continued random spasms in her arms, and impairments to her vision, hearing and speech. Her face needed extensive reconstruction surgery to repair the damage.

I was shocked when I watched this report on the TV news, and especially when I realized this horrific crime occurred just a few miles from where I had been pastoring at that time. But I was even more astonished to hear of Michelle Knight's courage, who unashamedly confessed her faith in God to the media, along with her forgiveness for this man who had done such evil against her.

In a YouTube video, in which all three women appeared after their rescue, Knight explained her decision to forgive her abuser. *"I don't want to be consumed by hatred... we need to take a leap of faith and know that God is in control. We have been hurt by people, but we need to rely on God as being the judge. God has a plan for all of us,"* she said.

I was deeply moved and utterly amazed. I shudder to think of the unspeakable horrors this young woman endured, and yet she came to terms with her need to forgive. Not because this man repented or deserved her forgiveness... but because she needed to survive, to rise above this tragedy and move on with her life.

Of whatever hurts or offenses I've experienced in my lifetime, none come remotely close to anything like what Michelle Knight endured. And if she was able to find forgiveness for such a sick, sadistic monster, surely you and I can forgive our offenders too.

Forgiveness is not about finding justice or getting even... it's about liberating yourself from the bondage of bitterness and resentment that can rot away your soul. It must begin with your willful decision to forgive, and then by continuing to reinforce that decision every day... relying on God's strength to carry it out, as long as it takes, until your recovery is complete.

Four Things to Help You to Forgive

(1) Redirect Blame for Your Offense Toward Your Real Enemy, Satan. As discussed in chapters 1 and 9, the Devil is your real adversary, not flesh and blood... neither the church nor your brothers or sisters in Christ. As the Apostle Paul wrote, *"For we do not wrestle against flesh and blood, but against principalities, against powers, against the rulers of the darkness of this age, against spiritual hosts of wickedness in the heavenly places" (Ephesians 6:12).*

Satan is the one who exploited you and others to orchestrate the ambush against you, and rightfully deserves your indignation and anger. His greatest desire is to destroy your soul... to upset you so effectively that you'll never return to church. His ambition is to alienate you from the spiritual strength, fellowship and ministry available there... and if possible, to tempt you into drifting away from your relationship with Christ entirely.

Paul pointed out who the real enemy was, to remind us that we can't hope to overcome him in our own strength, but that we have to rely on the Lord's power *(Ephesians*

6:10)... both to defeat the Devil, as well as to find mercy and forgiveness for those whom Satan has deceived and used to hurt us. *"And be kind to one another, tenderhearted, forgiving one another, just as God in Christ forgave you" (Ephesians 4:32).*

No, this does not exonerate the offender's responsibility from whatever sins or trespasses they may have committed against you. However this helps provide a rationale to overcome the unwillingness of your mind to allow thoughts of forgiveness. In other words, you may become more disposed to forgive your brother, because you realize, that you too have been a victim of Satan's exploits and manipulations.... and can empathize with similar struggles with the old sinful flesh *(Romans 3:23, Romans 7:15-20).*

By all means, don't allow Satan to win this victory over you, but reverse his advantage by forgiving those who have done you wrong. Forgiveness is the greatest weapon we have against hurts. It neutralizes the enemy's ability to manipulate us with anger and bitterness.

(2) Pray for Your Offenders. During an early time in my ministry, I was betrayed and deeply wounded by persons close to me... who neither repented nor sought reconciliation. And though I tried diligently to forgive, I struggled and failed... that is, until I began to practice what I had long-been preaching from Jesus' Sermon on the Mount. He said, "*...love your enemies, bless those who curse you, do good to those who hate you, and pray for those who spitefully use you and persecute you" (Matthew 5:44)*.

Even though I had already prayed occasionally for the ones who had wounded me (mostly, self-serving prayers, asking the Lord to vindicate me through their repentance), I started praying differently, as one sincerely concerned for their souls, asking Jesus to draw them to Him, to guide and help their lives. I prayed faithfully each day, and each time hurt or resentment crept up into my thoughts.

My offenders obviously needed the prayer, but not any more than I needed the opportunity to pray for them, and for God to change my attitude. In this case, I never knew whether they ever had a change of heart or not... I only hope for the best. However, after several weeks of this kind of prayer, I was amazed at the changes in me. I found myself growing more compassionate, merciful and forgiving, and eventually the hurt diminished to only a distant memory.

Since that time, I've seen how effective this kind of prayer has been to help others overcome their struggles to forgive. Not only does it make changes in the heart of the offended, but God can indeed work in the heart of the offender too.

(3) Clear Your Slate of Any Past-Due Accounts. One of the most prevalent hindrances with the ability to forgive, is the residue of "past" wounds or offences that still have never been dealt with or resolved. Unforgiven resentments that have been allowed to fester, sometimes over a period of many years, develop deep roots down into our soul... and can affect many aspects of one's life.

Such roots of bitterness will contribute to a sensitivity to offenses, and may be the cause for many more subsequent hurts and wounds. *"...looking carefully lest anyone fall short of the grace of God; lest any root of bitterness springing up cause trouble, and by this many become defiled" (Hebrews 12:14-15)*.

I've personally known adults who have carried hatred and bitterness toward an abusive parent since their childhood, who seethe and become hostile and flush-faced at the very mention of their parent's name. And unfortunately, these same people are often the ones who continue experiencing frequent hurts and wounds... because hurt people are more susceptible to additional hurts.

All bitterness is relative, and all forgiveness is relative. So in order to forgive your present offenders, it may be necessary to go back and forgive your offenders of the past. Pull out those troublesome bitter roots.... so that genuine healing and restoration can take place in your heart.

(4) Cast Your Burden on the Lord. The Bible teaches us that Christ's sufferings and atoning death on the cross, was to bear our griefs and carry our sorrows *(Isaiah 53:4)*. This not only means that he paid the penalty for sin and death in your behalf, but He also has taken your hurts, wounds and heartaches so that you can experience His promise of peace and rest. As Peter wrote, *"Cast all your care upon Him, for He cares for you" (1 Peter 5:7)*.

You've heard it said, and indeed it is so true, *"To err is human, to forgive is divine."* Forgiveness is not really something we can comprehend apart from the remarkable grace and mercy of God's love, in sending Jesus to die for us. And neither is it something we can hope to offer anyone else apart from God's enabling strength and power.

What we must do in response to our hurts, is the same thing as when we come to Christ to trust Him by faith for our salvation. We make a decision to forgive, based on our faith and obedience to God's Word. And even though we may continue to struggle for a time with feelings of hurt, we trust the Lord to carry those wounds for us, until such a time he can complete His healing in our heart.

Finally, in the book, *Landmines in the Path of the Believer*, Charles Stanley wrote these words of wisdom. *"We are to forgive so that we may enjoy God's goodness without feeling the weight of anger burning deep within* our hearts. Forgiveness does not mean we recant the fact that what happened to us was wrong. Instead, we roll our burdens onto the Lord and allow Him to carry them for us."

Here's a Suggested Prayer to Begin This Process:

"Dear Heavenly Father, I come to you in the name of Jesus, asking you to help me... and to bring healing to the wounds I've experienced. Forgive me for the bitterness that I have retained in my heart, as I don't want to remain resentful toward anyone. I choose to forgive my offenders, realizing they were deceived and exploited by our real enemy... and I pray for their soul, that you will bring their heart to repentance and restore our fellowship together in you. Please take this burden from my shoulders, and grant me your peace and rest. I ask these things in Jesus name."

We have a special passion to help believers and congregations who deal with these issues. If we can pray with you, come speak at your church, or help in any way, please contact us at www.victorious.org.

www.ingramcontent.com/pod-product-compliance
Lightning Source LLC
Chambersburg PA
CBHW071517040426
42444CB00008B/1688